JOYFUL LIVING IN CHRIST

A Study in Philippians

ROBERT GRIFFITH

GRACE AND TRUTH PUBLISHING
PO Box 338, Gunnedah NSW 2380 Australia
www.graceandtruthpublishing.com.au

ISBN 978-1-7635504-7-6

TABLE OF CONTENTS

1. CONFIDENT BEGINNINGS

Philippians 1:1-11 *"Paul and Timothy, servants of Christ Jesus, to all God's holy people in Christ Jesus at Philippi, together with the overseers and deacons: Grace and peace to you from God our Father and the Lord Jesus Christ. I thank my God every time I remember you. In all my prayers for all of you, I always pray with joy because of your partnership in the gospel from the first day until now, being confident of this, that he who began a good work in you will carry it on to completion until the day of Christ Jesus.*

It is right for me to feel this way about all of you, since I have you in my heart and, whether I am in chains or defending and confirming the gospel, all of you share in God's grace with me. God can testify how I long for all of you with the affection of Christ Jesus.

And this is my prayer: that your love may abound more and more in knowledge and depth of insight, so that you may be able to discern what is best and may be pure and blameless for the day of Christ, filled with the fruit of righteousness that comes through Jesus Christ - to the glory and praise of God."

Introduction: A Letter from Lockdown

The letter to the Philippians is a remarkable gift to the church. It's not written from a place of comfort or peace, but from prison. The Apostle Paul, likely in Rome, is writing under house arrest, uncertain of his future.

Yet his tone is not filled with bitterness or despair - it overflows with joy, thanksgiving, and confidence in Christ. This is no small thing. It reminds us that joy is not rooted in circumstances, but in relationship.

Philippians teaches us what it means to live joyfully, confidently, and purposefully - even in hard places.

In Philippians 1:1–11, we find Paul's opening greeting and prayer. These words set the tone for the entire letter. In them, we find key themes that will guide the rest of our study: identity in Christ, the joy of Christian fellowship, the assurance of God's ongoing work in us, and the call to grow in love and spiritual discernment. We will be exploring these verses under the title *'Confident Beginnings.'* Here, Paul invites us to see the Christian life not as a burdensome duty, but as a joyful journey which God Himself began and promises to complete.

1. Our Identity in Christ (v.1–2)

Paul opens with a customary greeting, yet every word is rich with meaning. *"Paul and Timothy, servants of Christ Jesus."* The Greek word used here is *doulos*, meaning *'slave'* or *'bondservant.'* Paul does not assert his apostolic authority, though he could. Instead, he introduces himself as a servant - someone whose life is completely surrendered to the will of another. This sets the tone for everything that follows. Christian life and leadership are built not on control or personal achievement, but on submission to Christ.

He writes *"to all God's holy people in Christ Jesus at Philippi."* The term *"holy people"* (*hagios*) means *'set apart.'* These believers are not perfect, but they are set apart by God's grace. Their holiness is not based on their performance but on their position in Christ. This reminds us of our identity as believers - not as consumers or critics of the church, but as God's chosen, loved and set apart for His purposes.

Paul also greets the *"overseers and deacons,"* acknowledging the church's leadership. This is one of the only places in Paul's letters where he mentions church leaders in the greeting.

It suggests that Philippi was a well-established church with structure, yet his greeting remains inclusive - *"all God's holy people."* Leaders and laypeople alike are united under the same grace. He offers them *"grace and peace from God our Father and the Lord Jesus Christ."* Grace, the empowering presence of God, is the foundation of the Christian life. Peace is the result of that grace: peace with God, peace within, and peace with others. These two words summarize the heart of the gospel. They're not just nice sentiments; they're transformative realities that reshape how we live and relate to one another.

2. Thanksgiving Rooted in Relationship (v.3-5)

Then Paul writes, *"I thank my God every time I remember you."* This is a very powerful statement. Every remembrance of this church prompts thanksgiving. Even from prison, Paul's heart is filled with gratitude. He doesn't focus on what he lacks or the injustice of his imprisonment. Instead, he focuses on the joy of gospel fellowship.

He continues: *"In all my prayers for all of you, I always pray with joy because of your partnership in the gospel from the first day until now."* The Greek word translated *"partnership"* is actually *koinonia*. It implies deep fellowship and shared mission. The Philippians were not spectators in ministry; they were active participants. They supported Paul financially, prayed for him faithfully, and identified with him even in times of trial.

What a model for the church today. True fellowship is not just polite greetings on Sunday mornings and sharing morning tea … it is a deep and enduring partnership in the mission of the gospel. It involves generosity, prayer, and sacrifice. When we lock arms with one another to advance the kingdom, our relationships deepen and our joy then multiplies.

Notice how Paul's gratitude is tied to their ongoing commitment: *"from the first day until now."* The Philippians weren't enthusiastic for a moment and then distracted. They were consistent. This is the kind of partnership that sustains ministry - not flash-in-the-pan enthusiasm, but an enduring faithfulness.

3. Confidence in God's Ongoing Work (v.6)

Paul then makes one of the most beloved declarations in the New Testament: *"being confident of this, that he who began a good work in you will carry it on to completion until the day of Christ Jesus."* This is the foundation of our assurance. The *"good work"* refers to the work of salvation and sanctification - the moment God awakened their hearts to believe in Christ, and the ongoing process of making them more like Him. Paul's confidence is not in the Philippians' strength or in their willpower, but in God's unwavering faithfulness.

This verse is a great encouragement to every believer who has ever doubted their spiritual progress. Growth in grace is often quite slow. Setbacks come. We struggle with sin, discouragement, and distractions. But the work God begins, He finishes. He is not a careless builder or a distracted artist. He will always complete what He starts.

This promise does not make our efforts irrelevant. Instead, it fuels our perseverance. Because God is working in us, we can keep moving forward with hope. The Spirit of God is at work within us, shaping our character and guiding our steps until the day we stand complete in Christ.

4. Gospel Bonds Forged Through Suffering (v.7–8)

Paul continues his thought in verse 7: *"It is right for me to feel this way about all of you, since I have you in my heart. For whether I am in chains or defending and confirming the gospel, all of you share in God's grace with me."*

Here, Paul expresses both the emotional and theological connection he has with the Philippians. His affection isn't sentimental or shallow - it's rooted in shared mission and mutual suffering. Whether he is in prison *("in chains")* or out in the world defending and proclaiming the gospel, the Philippians have remained spiritually and emotionally invested. They *"share in God's grace"* with him - a powerful phrase that unites them under one mission and one Saviour.

Paul is not speaking of grace in the general sense here, but of a specific grace: the grace of ministry, the grace of enduring suffering for the sake of the gospel, and the grace that sustains and binds Christian communities together. The Philippians have been generous toward Paul, supportive in his trials, and unwavering in their spiritual solidarity.

This speaks volumes about what the church is meant to be. We are not merely an audience gathered around a preacher. We are fellow workers, fellow sufferers, and fellow recipients of divine grace. Ministry is never meant to be a solo endeavour. It is shared, multiplied, and sustained by a community bound together in love and empowered by grace.

Then Paul writes in verse 8: *"God can testify how I long for all of you with the affection of Christ Jesus."* This is a staggering statement. Paul appeals to God as his witness - underscoring the depth and sincerity of his love. But even more remarkably, he says he longs for them with *"the affection of Christ Jesus."* This is not merely Paul's personal affection; it is Christ's affection expressed through Paul.

Here we see one of the profound truths of Christian transformation: as we mature in Christ, His love begins to flow through us. Our affections become more like His.

Our love becomes more sacrificial, more patient, more pure. Paul's deep bond with the Philippians is a glimpse into what it looks like to love others with the very heart of Christ. This raises a question for us today: is our love for the church marked by the affection of Christ? Are we willing to invest emotionally and spiritually in our fellow believers, to love with patience, humility, and sacrifice?

5. A Prayer for Abounding Love and Discernment (v.9)

Paul now turns from thanksgiving and affirmation to intercession. He writes in verse 9: *"And this is my prayer: that your love may abound more and more in knowledge and depth of insight."*

This is not a vague wish for people to be nicer. It is a very specific prayer for spiritual growth - that their love would not only increase in volume *("abound more and more")* but also in depth and wisdom. Biblical love is not blind or sentimental. It is discerning. It seeks what is best, not what is easiest. It pursues truth and purity, not mere emotional connection.

The Greek used here is important. *"Knowledge"* (*epignōsis*) refers to deep, spiritual understanding - the kind of knowledge that leads to intimacy with God and wise living. *"Depth of insight"* refers to moral perception - the ability to see beyond appearances and grasp what truly honours God.

Paul is praying that their love would be intelligent, informed, and insightful - a love shaped by the gospel and rooted in truth. This is especially relevant today, where "love" is often used to excuse compromise or avoid confrontation. But biblical love does not ignore sin or dismiss truth; it seeks what is best for others, even when that is hard.

6. Discernment That Leads to Holiness (v.10)

Paul continues: *"... so that you may be able to discern what is best and may be pure and blameless for the day of Christ."* The goal of this abounding love and spiritual insight is moral clarity and godly living. Paul is praying that the Philippians would be able to make wise choices - to *"discern what is best."* This goes beyond avoiding sin. It means pursuing what is most excellent, what is most glorifying to God.

Many Christians ask, *"What's wrong with this?"* as a way of justifying morally ambiguous choices. But a better question is, *"What is best?"* What choice most reflects Christ? What course of action most advances the gospel? What decision produces holiness and joy?

The aim is to be *"pure and blameless"* - to live a life marked by sincerity and integrity, free from moral stain. The word "pure" implies internal authenticity – that is, being the same in private as in public. *"Blameless"* implies living in such a way that no legitimate accusation can be brought against us. And Paul points this toward a specific moment in time: *"the day of Christ."* This is the day of Christ's return, when all will be revealed and judged. Paul wants the Philippians to live in light of that day - to pursue lives of holiness not just for their own benefit, but in preparation for meeting their Saviour face to face.

7. Fruitfulness That Glorifies God (v.11)

Finally, Paul completes his prayer with a picture of gospel fruitfulness: *"... filled with the fruit of righteousness that comes through Jesus Christ - to the glory and praise of God."* This is the end goal of Paul's intercession - that their lives would be full of righteousness. Not a self-righteousness that comes from legalism or effort, but the fruit of righteousness that flows from union with Christ.

The metaphor of fruit is important. Fruit grows naturally from a healthy tree. It's the visible evidence of life. Likewise, the righteous actions of believers are the evidence of a life rooted in Christ. These fruits - love, purity, wisdom, humility, service - are not produced by trying harder, but by abiding deeper in Jesus. And ultimately, this is not about self-improvement or public praise. It is *to the glory and praise of God.*" When our lives reflect Christ, God is glorified. When the church is holy, the world sees the beauty of the gospel.

8. Living with the End in View

Paul's prayer ends with a vision - not just of what the Philippians should do, but of who they are becoming. He wants them to be ready for *"the day of Christ,"* to live with the final judgment and ultimate hope in view.

That day is not only a moment of accounting, but a moment of glory. It's the day when Christ returns, when His work in us will be completed, and when our lives will be fully aligned with His purpose.

In the Christian life, how we live today is shaped by what we believe about tomorrow. Paul was always mindful of the future. He lived with a deep awareness that this life was temporary and that eternity was real. That's why he didn't waste time on petty arguments or selfish ambition. That's why joy mattered to him, even in prison. That's why he prayed for his friends to grow in wisdom, love, and holiness.

Living with the end in view means making decisions based not just on what is easy or popular, but on what will matter when we stand before Christ. It means choosing purity over compromise, truth over comfort, and kingdom priorities over worldly pursuits.

This doesn't mean we must live in fear. Quite the opposite. Because of God's faithfulness, we live with confidence. He who began a good work in us will complete it. That's not just a comforting thought - it's a solid promise that fuels perseverance, hope, and joy.

9. Confident Beginnings and Lasting Joy

Let's return to the overall theme of this chapter: 'Confident Beginnings.' Paul's joy and confidence does not come from his own success or the Philippians' performance. It comes from the knowledge that God is at work.

Every "good work" begins with God's initiative and ends with God's completion. This includes the work of salvation, sanctification, and spiritual fruitfulness.

So much anxiety in the Christian life comes from forgetting this truth. We think it all depends on us. We become discouraged when we stumble, or fearful that we'll never grow. But Philippians 1:6 reminds us that God is not a quitter. He finishes what He starts. He is not just the *Author* of our faith; He is also the *Finisher* (Hebrews 12:2).

This truth transforms how we view our failures and fears. If God began the work in us, and He has promised to finish it, then we can rest - not in passivity, but in peace. We work out our salvation with reverence (Philippians 2:12) but always knowing that *"it is God who works in us to will and to act according to His good purpose."* (Philippians 2:13).

Joy flows from this confidence. Paul prays with joy. He remembers with joy. He writes with joy - even from prison - because he knows God is at work. When we see life through this lens, joy is not dependent on outcomes but on the ongoing activity of God in us.

10. Application for Today's Church

So, how can we apply Philippians 1:1–11 to our lives and to our churches today? Let's consider a few ways we can live out the truth within this passage:

➢ *Embrace Your Identity as a Servant:* to Christ. Whether you are a pastor, a parent, a teacher, a retiree, or a student - if you belong to Christ, you are His servant. Live for His will, not your own.

➢ *Cultivate Gospel Partnerships:* Church is not a spectator sport. Paul rejoiced in the Philippians because they partnered with him in the gospel. They gave, prayed, and stood with him. Ask yourself: am I actively partnering in the mission of Christ? Am I giving, serving, encouraging, and standing with others?

➢ *Trust God's Ongoing Work in You:* Spiritual growth is often messy and slow. But God is faithful. Don't lose heart when progress feels hard. He is still working in you. Keep seeking Him in prayer, Scripture, and community, and trust that He will finish the work He started.

➢ *Let Christ's Love Shape Your Relationships:* Paul loved the Philippians with *"the affection of Christ Jesus."* We are called to love one another with that same love - deep, sacrificial, patient, and pure. What would change in our churches if we related to each other like that?

➢ *Pray for Growth in Love and Discernment:* Paul didn't just pray for comfort or safety. He prayed for spiritual depth. Are you praying for that kind of growth - in yourself and others? Ask God to help your love abound in wisdom and to make you pure and blameless for Christ.

➤ *Live in Light of the Day of Christ:* Live today as if Christ were returning tomorrow. Pursue what is best, what is holy, what glorifies God. Let the certainty of Christ's return shape your decisions, your desires, and your direction.

Conclusion

As we close this first chapter, we return to Paul's central conviction: God began a good work in us, and He will finish it. That promise isn't just theology - it's fuel for the journey. It means we are never alone, never abandoned, never unfinished. It means every trial, every joy, every act of obedience is part of something God is doing in us and through us.

Let this fill you with joy today. Let it drive out fear. Let it call you to faithfulness and hope. The Christian life is not a desperate attempt to please God in our own strength. It's a confident journey, anchored in grace, carried by love, and destined for glory.

Let us, like Paul, pray with joy for one another - that our love may abound, our faith may grow, and our lives may bear fruit that glorifies God.

2. CHRIST IS PREACHED

Philippians 1:12-26 *"Now I want you to know, brothers and sisters, that what has happened to me has actually served to advance the gospel. As a result, it has become clear throughout the whole palace guard and to everyone else that I am in chains for Christ. And because of my chains, most of the brothers and sisters have become confident in the Lord and dare all the more to proclaim the gospel without fear.*

It is true that some preach Christ out of envy and rivalry, but others out of goodwill. The latter do so out of love, knowing that I am put here for the defence of the gospel. The former preach Christ out of selfish ambition, not sincerely, supposing that they can stir up trouble for me while I am in chains. But what does it matter? The important thing is that in every way, whether from false motives or true, Christ is preached. And because of this I rejoice.

Yes, and I will continue to rejoice, for I know that through your prayers and God's provision of the Spirit of Jesus Christ what has happened to me will turn out for my deliverance. I eagerly expect and hope that I will in no way be ashamed but will have sufficient courage so that now as always Christ will be exalted in my body, whether by life or by death. For to me, to live is Christ and to die is gain. If I am to go on living in the body, this will mean fruitful labour for me.

Yet what shall I choose? I do not know! I am torn between the two: I desire to depart and be with Christ, which is better by far; but it is more necessary for you that I remain in the body. Convinced of this, I know that I will remain, and I will continue with all of you for your progress and joy in the faith, so that through my being with you again your boasting in Christ Jesus will abound on account of me."

Introduction: Joy in Unlikely Places

The Apostle Paul is in prison, and his future is anything but clear. He is chained, isolated, and facing the possibility of execution. Most people in his situation would be anxious, angry, or depressed. But Paul is filled with joy and purpose. Why? Because Paul is not focused on his personal comfort or security - he is focused on Christ being glorified. As long as Christ is preached, Paul rejoices. As long as Christ is magnified in his life or his death, Paul is content.

In Philippians 1:12–26, Paul lifts the curtain on his present circumstances, not to ask for pity, but instead testify to the triumph of the gospel. In these verses, we see a man whose identity is so rooted in Christ that suffering only deepens his joy.

Paul's imprisonment has not hindered the gospel - it has advanced it. And whether he lives or dies, his one aim remains clear: to exalt Christ.

This passage gives us a powerful vision for what it means to live for Christ. It challenges our assumptions about success, suffering, and significance. It calls us to a joy that is not rooted in ease, but in eternal purpose. And it invites us to declare with Paul, *"For to me, to live is Christ and to die is gain."*

1. The Gospel Advances Through Opposition (vv.12–14)

Paul begins with a surprising claim: *"Now I want you to know, brothers and sisters, that what has happened to me has actually served to advance the gospel."*

From a human perspective, Paul's imprisonment could seem like a major setback for the gospel. After all, Paul was the church's most effective missionary and church planter. Now he is stuck in Rome, under guard.

Paul sees things differently. His chains have not confined the gospel - they have propelled it forward. The Greek word translated *'advance'* (*prokopēn*) describes an army moving through difficult terrain by clearing obstacles. Paul is saying, *"My imprisonment is clearing new ground for the gospel."* What looked like a barrier was actually a bridge. God is using hardship to open new doors. How is the gospel advancing? Paul explains: *"As a result, it has become clear throughout the whole palace guard and to everyone else that I am in chains for Christ."* (v.13)

Paul's imprisonment has brought him into contact with the elite Roman guard - men who would have never heard the gospel otherwise. Paul is not sulking in his cell; he is sharing the gospel with his captors. And the result is that the message of Christ is spreading even in Caesar's household. This reminds us that God's mission is not limited by our circumstances. The gospel does not stop when we suffer. In fact, it often shines more brightly through adversity. Our witness is most powerful when it is costly.

Paul continues: *"And because of my chains, most of the brothers and sisters have become confident in the Lord and dare all the more to proclaim the gospel without fear."* (v.14) Paul's courage has inspired others. His imprisonment is not causing believers to retreat in fear - it's emboldening them to speak up. Suffering for the gospel can be contagious in the best way. When others see us remain faithful in trials, they are strengthened in their own faith.

This is the paradox of the kingdom of God: when the church is persecuted, very often it grows. When the messenger is imprisoned, the message spreads. God delights in turning the enemy's plans upside down. And Paul rejoices in this - not because he enjoys the pain, but because he sees God's purpose in it.

2. Rejoicing When Christ Is Preached (vv.15–18)

Paul now shifts to a surprising development: not all gospel preaching is done from pure motives. *"It is true that some preach Christ out of envy and rivalry, but others out of goodwill."* (v.15) Apparently, some individuals in Rome – very likely Christian preachers - are using Paul's imprisonment as an opportunity to elevate themselves. They are preaching Christ, but their motives are mixed. They are not really false teachers - they're preaching the true gospel - but they are doing so to compete with Paul, not to honour Christ.

Paul elaborates: *"The latter do so out of love, knowing that I am put here for the defence of the gospel. The former preach Christ out of selfish ambition, not sincerely, supposing that they can stir up trouble for me while I am in chains."* (vv.16–17). There are two groups: one preaches Christ out of love and support for Paul's mission; the other preaches out of envy and ambition. They think that by outshining Paul while he's locked away, they will gain influence and cause Paul distress.

This situation could easily provoke bitterness and even resentment. After all, Paul has sacrificed everything for the gospel. He has poured himself out in love and labour, only to be undercut by ambitious preachers seeking to build their own platforms. But Paul's response is breathtaking in its humility: *"But what does it matter? The important thing is that in every way, whether from false motives or true, Christ is preached. And because of this I rejoice."* (v.18) Paul's ego is not at stake - Christ's glory is. As long as the true gospel is being preached, Paul rejoices, even if he personally suffers. His focus is not on his reputation but on Christ's proclamation. That is true gospel maturity.

How often are we tempted to critique others' ministries based on style, personality, or popularity? But Paul reminds us: the central question is this: *is Christ being preached?*

We can and should care about doctrine and integrity, but we must also check our hearts. Are we more concerned with Christ being known or with ourselves being noticed? This verse is an invitation to let go of comparison, envy, and competition. Gospel ministry is not a race for recognition. It is a collective mission to make Jesus known. And if Christ is preached - even by people with impure motives - that is cause for rejoicing.

3. Christ Will Be Exalted in My Body (vv.18b–20)

Paul moves from present joy to future hope: *"Yes, and I will continue to rejoice, for I know that through your prayers and God's provision of the Spirit of Jesus Christ what has happened to me will turn out for my deliverance."* (vv.18b–19) Even in prison, Paul is confident. He doesn't know whether he will live or die, but he knows that God will be glorified.

The word *"deliverance"* here (*sōtēria*) can mean salvation, vindication, or rescue - it's intentionally ambiguous. Paul is not claiming certainty of physical release, but of spiritual triumph.

And how is Paul sustained? Two sources: the prayers of the Philippians and the provision of the Spirit of Jesus Christ. This is a beautiful reminder that gospel ministry is not individualistic. Paul depends on the prayers of others and the power of the Holy Spirit. Even the great Apostle needs the intercession of fellow believers and the sustaining grace of God.

Then Paul shares the passion that governs his life: *"I eagerly expect and hope that I will in no way be ashamed but will have sufficient courage so that now as always Christ will be exalted in my body, whether by life or by death."* (v.20) This is the heart of the passage. Paul's greatest desire is not comfort, freedom, or even survival.

It is that Christ would be exalted in his body - through life or death. The word here *"exalted"* (*megalynthēsetai*) means to magnify, to make great. Paul wants Christ to be seen as glorious, no matter what happens to him.

What an extraordinary mindset. Most of us pray to be rescued from difficulty. Paul prays to have courage in difficulty so that Christ is magnified. Whether through continued ministry or martyrdom, Paul's goal is the same - to make Jesus look glorious.

This challenges us deeply. What do we live for? What do we fear losing? What are we most eager for? If our aim is to magnify Christ - not ourselves - then suffering can actually become an opportunity for witness. Our pain becomes a platform for praise. Our trials then become a stage for His triumph.

4. The Christian's Paradox: Life and Death Reframed (vv.21–22)

Paul now offers one of the most quoted and powerful summaries of Christian identity in the entire New Testament: *"For to me, to live is Christ and to die is gain."* (v.21) This statement is astonishing. For most people, death is the ultimate loss. It is the end of all dreams, relationships, and opportunities. But not for Paul. Because his life is rooted in Christ, death is not defeat - it's promotion. Let's break this down.

"To live is Christ…"

Paul does not mean merely believing in Christ or serving Christ - he means Christ is the very content and purpose of his life. Every breath, every decision, every goal revolves around knowing Christ, serving Christ, and making Christ known.

His entire existence is Christ-centred. Christ is not just a compartment of Paul's life; Christ *is* Paul's life. This kind of statement doesn't come from religious obligation - it comes from deep affection and intimate relationship.

Paul loves Jesus so much, treasures Him so highly, that all of life is a joyful response to His grace. Work, suffering, travel, writing, preaching - all of it is *"Christ."* Can we say the same? For many, life is defined by career, family, hobbies, health, or possessions. These things are not wrong, but they are not ultimate. For Paul, Christ is the reason he lives, and everything else is secondary.

"...and to die is gain."

How can death be gain? Only if what lies ahead is better than what lies behind. For Paul, death is not the end - it's the beginning of being with Christ in a fuller, more direct way. In verse 23, he says he desires *"to depart and be with Christ, which is better by far."* Death brings him face to face with the One he loves most.

This radically reorients our view of suffering, aging, and mortality. The Christian doesn't cling to life with desperation because death is not separation from what we value most - it is union with Him. Paul's hope makes him fearless. Whether his earthly life continues or ends, he sees gain either way. *"If I am to go on living in the body, this will mean fruitful labour for me. Yet what shall I choose? I do not know!"* (v.22) Paul sees both options - life and death - as filled with purpose. If he lives, he labours. If he dies, he gains Christ fully.

It's a win-win situation. He's torn, not because of fear, but because he values both gospel ministry and the presence of Christ. This tension is beautiful.

Paul doesn't have a death wish, nor does he idolize comfort. His only desire is to glorify Christ, whether in the present body or in eternal presence.

5. Living for the Joy and Progress of Others (vv.23–26)

Paul continues his reflection: *"I am torn between the two: I desire to depart and be with Christ, which is better by far; but it is more necessary for you that I remain in the body."* (vv.23–24).

This reveals Paul's pastoral heart. Though his personal desire is to be with Christ, he chooses to stay if it benefits the Philippians' spiritual growth. His life is not his own. It belongs to Christ, and therefore, to Christ's people. Ministry is more important than personal desire.

"Convinced of this, I know that I will remain, and I will continue with all of you for your progress and joy in the faith." (v.25). Paul is confident that God still has work for him to do - specifically, helping the Philippians grow in faith and joy.

Notice again the theme of joy. Joy is not a peripheral feeling for Paul - it is central to the Christian life. His ministry is not about behaviour modification, but heart transformation that produces joy in Christ.

"So that through my being with you again your boasting in Christ Jesus will abound on account of me." (v.26)

The ultimate goal is not Paul's reputation, but Christ's glory. Paul wants the Philippians to grow in joyful faith so that they will exalt Christ even more. This is a beautiful vision for discipleship: not just knowledge, but joy that overflows into praise.

What does this mean for us? It means …

> *our lives are not our own.* We live for the good of others and the glory of Christ.

> *our suffering is not meaningless.* Even when circumstances are hard, God is using us to strengthen others.

> *our joy is not circumstantial.* Like Paul, we can rejoice in prison, in illness, in uncertainty, because our joy is in Christ - not comfort.

6. What It Means to Say, *"To live is Christ"*

Let's return to Paul's wonderful declaration: *"To live is Christ."* What would that look like if we believed it and lived it?

> It means **Christ is the source** of our life. We were dead in sin, but now we are alive in Him.

> It means **Christ is the goal** of our life. Every decision, every desire, every dream is surrendered to His will.

> It means **Christ is the strength** of our life. We do not labour in our own power, but by His Spirit within us.

> It means **Christ is the joy** of our life. Our ultimate satisfaction is not in success, relationships, or pleasures, but in Him.

> It means **Christ is the reward** at the end of our life. We live now with eyes on eternity, knowing that death is gain only because Christ is there.

"To live is Christ" is a radical redefinition of life. It calls us away from self-centeredness, away from fear, away from temporary pursuits - and invites us into a life of eternal purpose, deep joy, and fearless love.

Conclusion:

Philippians 1:12–26 gives us a breathtaking portrait of gospel-centred living.

Paul's joy in prison, his freedom from rivalry, his courage in suffering, and his longing for Christ - all flow from one central reality: Jesus is everything. This is not a call to imitate Paul in our own strength. It is a call to surrender fully to Christ, who lives in us by His Spirit.

It is Christ who gives us the boldness to witness in adversity, the humility to rejoice when others succeed, and the courage to face death without fear.

Let us ask God to help us make Paul's words our own: *"For to me, to live is Christ and to die is gain."* May we live with purpose, suffer with joy, and die with hope - all because Christ is preached, and Christ is glorified.

3. STANDING FIRM IN CHRIST

Philippians 1:27-30 *"Whatever happens, conduct yourselves in a manner worthy of the gospel of Christ. Then, whether I come and see you or only hear about you in my absence, I will know that you stand firm in the one Spirit, striving together as one for the faith of the gospel without being frightened in any way by those who oppose you. This is a sign to them that they will be destroyed, but that you will be saved - and that by God. For it has been granted to you on behalf of Christ not only to believe in him, but also to suffer for him, since you are going through the same struggle you saw I had, and now hear that I still have."*

Introduction: Living in a Way That Reflects the Gospel

As we return to Paul's letter to the Philippians, we come to a pivotal moment. Paul has just reflected on his personal situation - imprisoned, uncertain of the future, yet joyfully confident that Christ will be exalted in his life or death. Now, beginning in verse 27, he turns his focus outward to the Philippian believers. What follows is not merely encouragement - it is a call to arms. Paul urges the church to live lives *"worthy of the gospel of Christ."*

This is a very powerful and challenging phrase. It does not mean we earn the gospel or somehow prove ourselves deserving of it. Rather, it means that our lives should reflect the transforming power and supreme value of the gospel. If we claim to believe in Jesus - crucified, risen, and reigning - then our conduct should mirror His grace, truth, and courage. Paul is calling the church to unity, to perseverance, and to boldness in suffering. He writes not from a place of ease but from chains. Yet his expectation is firm: no matter what happens to him - whether he lives or dies - the church must live faithfully and fearlessly. Let us listen closely to his words, because they speak directly to us today.

In a culture increasingly indifferent or hostile to Christian faith, how we live matters. The world is watching. More importantly, our Lord is watching. Will we live lives worthy of the gospel? Will we stand firm in Christ? Will we face opposition with joy?

1. Conduct That Reflects the Gospel (v.27a)

Paul begins with a foundational exhortation: *"Whatever happens, conduct yourselves in a manner worthy of the gospel of Christ."* (v.27a) The Greek word for *"conduct"* (*politeuesthe*) comes from the root word *polis*, meaning city. It has the sense of fulfilling your duty as a citizen.

This is a deliberate word choice, especially for Philippians. Philippi was a Roman colony, and its citizens were proud of their Roman identity and privileges. Paul is reminding them - and also us - that they belong to a higher Kingdom. Their primary citizenship is not Roman - it is heavenly. And as citizens of heaven, they must live accordingly.

This is a theme Paul returns to in Philippians 3:20: *"But our citizenship is in heaven."* So when he calls the church to live *"worthy of the gospel,"* he is calling them to live as citizens of heaven in a world that does not acknowledge their King. To live worthy of the gospel means to live in such a way that our lives commend the gospel to others. It means integrity in our behaviour, purity in our relationships, humility in our speech, and consistency in our witness.

It means that when people look at us - how we speak, serve, forgive, and endure - they see something that makes them wonder about the One we follow. It's important to note what Paul doesn't say. He doesn't say, *"Only when life is going well,"* or *"Only when I visit you,"* or *"Only when your church is growing."* He says, *"Whatever happens…"*

Whether Paul is released or executed, whether the church is praised or persecuted - the conduct of their lives must remain consistent with the gospel.

This challenges us today. We live in a time of shifting values and moral confusion. It is tempting to compromise, to blend in, or to retreat into silence. But Paul calls us to courageous consistency.

The gospel is not just a belief we hold - it is a life we live. So ask yourself: Does your speech reflect the grace of Christ? Does your behaviour point people to His truth? Do your priorities demonstrate that you treasure Jesus above all? To live worthy of the gospel is not perfection - it is direction. It is a life centred on Christ and shaped by His cross.

2. Standing Firm in One Spirit (v.27b)

Paul continues: *"Then, whether I come and see you or only hear about you in my absence, I will know that you stand firm in the one Spirit…"* (v.27b) Paul longs to hear that the Philippians are standing firm - whether he is released or not. His concern is not for his own comfort, but for their faithfulness. And the first sign of a life worthy of the gospel is spiritual stability.

To *"stand firm"* is a military term. It means to hold your ground, not retreating in the face of the enemy. In a spiritual sense, it means not wavering in your faith, even when pressured by culture, persecution, or temptation. But Paul adds a crucial phrase: *"in the one Spirit."*

He is not urging them to dig deep into their own determination, but to rely on the Spirit of God. Christian firmness is not stubbornness - it is really Spirit-empowered endurance.

In Ephesians 6, Paul uses the same image when describing the armour of God: *"Stand firm, then…."* We are called to resist the devil, not in our strength, but with the armour and power God supplies. In our context, standing firm may mean:

➢ Holding to biblical truth when it's unpopular
➢ Maintaining sexual integrity in a permissive culture
➢ Refusing to retaliate when wronged
➢ Remaining joyful when circumstances are hard
➢ Continuing to serve when it feels thankless

We don't stand alone. We stand *in the Spirit* - the same Spirit Who raised Jesus from the dead and now lives in us. Paul's desire is that the Philippians - and all believers - will not buckle under pressure, but stand immovable, unashamed, and unafraid.

3. Striving Side by Side for the Faith of the Gospel (v.27c)

After urging the Philippians to conduct themselves in a manner worthy of the gospel and to stand firm in one Spirit, Paul adds another vital expression of gospel-centred living: *"…striving together as one for the faith of the gospel…"*

This image complements *"standing firm."* Not only must believers stand their ground, but they must also move forward together. The Christian life is not passive. It involves striving - a word that implies effort, struggle, and intentional movement. But this striving is not solitary - it is shared.

The word translated *"striving together"* (*sunathlountes*) is an athletic term, from which we get our English word *"athletics."* It evokes the picture of a team working in harmony toward a common goal - like rowers pulling in unison or runners pacing one another in a relay.

The goal, Paul says, is *"the faith of the gospel"* - the message of salvation in Christ that we have believed and now proclaim. This raises an important truth: the church is not a collection of individuals pursuing private spirituality - it is a unified body engaged in one shared mission. Gospel advancement is a team effort. We don't merely strive for personal holiness; we strive together to make Christ known and to defend the truth of the gospel in a world full of confusion and opposition.

So what does this striving look like in practice?

> It looks like believers **praying together** and for each other in times of difficulty.

> It looks like **serving together**, each using their gifts to build up the body.

> It looks like **bearing one another's burdens**, always encouraging the discouraged, restoring the fallen, and forgiving the offender.

> It looks like **proclaiming the gospel together**, which means supporting evangelism and missions with prayer, finances, and participation.

> It looks like **teaching and defending sound doctrine**, holding fast to biblical truth.

But for this to happen, we must be united - *"striving together as one."* Paul emphasises the importance of unity. Division kills momentum. When churches are fractured by gossip, pride, or preference, their gospel witness is weakened. Unity does not mean uniformity - we may all differ in personalities, backgrounds, or opinions - but we must be united in purpose and heart. The Philippians were already experiencing some internal tensions (as we'll see later in chapter 4). Paul knew that a divided church would rarely be able to withstand external pressure.

So he pleads for a kind of spiritual teamwork that is rooted in love, guided by truth, and aimed at gospel mission. This kind of unity requires humility, patience, and sacrificial love. It means we care more about Christ being exalted than about being right. It means we value the mission more than our own preferences. It means we are willing to forgive quickly and pursue peace diligently.

The church that strives together for the faith of the gospel is a powerful witness. In a fractured world, a unified church shines brightly. When the world sees believers loving one another, serving together, and standing with courage and compassion, they get a glimpse of Christ Himself.

4. Fearless in the Face of Opposition (v.28)

Paul continues his charge with another bold command: *"...without being frightened in any way by those who oppose you."* (v.28a) The word *"frightened"* here refers to a kind of panic - like a startled horse bolting in fear. Paul is saying, *"Do not be alarmed. Do not be intimidated. Do not let fear paralyse your faith."* The gospel will be opposed. That is guaranteed. But believers are not to cower.

Opposition comes in many forms. For the Philippians, it likely included social exclusion, slander, legal penalties, and perhaps even physical harm. For many Christians today, persecution still includes imprisonment, beatings, and death. For us, opposition may be more subtle - ridicule, marginalization, loss of opportunities, or pressure to compromise. Regardless of the form, Paul says: *"Do not be frightened. Stand firm. Strive together. Let your courage be a testimony."*

He continues: *"This is a sign to them that they will be destroyed, but that you will be saved - and that by God."* (v.28b) This is a difficult but powerful verse.

Paul is saying that the fearless courage of believers in the face of persecution is a sign - a sign of judgment for their opponents and a sign of salvation for themselves. Let's unpack this.

First, the bold witness of Christians under fire reveals the reality and power of their faith. When believers face hatred with love, suffering with joy, and loss with peace, the world takes notice. Their courage confirms that they belong to God and that the gospel is true.

Second, this courage also serves as a warning to opponents. It signals that their rebellion against God will not succeed. While they may be thinking they are winning - silencing Christians, mocking faith, or marginalizing the church - they are actually opposing the sovereign Lord, and that will not end well.

This is not a call to arrogance or vengeance. It's a reminder that our boldness speaks volumes, both to those being saved and to those who resist the truth. But notice one more phrase: *"and that by God."*

Salvation is not earned by courage - it is confirmed by it. The ultimate assurance comes not from our strength, but from God's saving grace. Our fearlessness in suffering is not the cause of our salvation but the fruit of it. So when opposition comes - and it will - we must remember that God is with us, God is for us, and God will finish what He began in us.

5. Suffering as a Gift and a Sign of Belonging (1:29–30)

Paul's words in verses 29 and 30 challenge our natural instincts and cultural expectations: *"For it has been granted to you on behalf of Christ not only to believe in him, but also to suffer for him, since you are going through the same struggle you saw I had, and now hear that I still have."*

At first glance, suffering is something most people try to avoid. We tend to think of faith as a source of comfort, peace, and blessing. Yet Paul flips this on its head. He teaches us that suffering for Christ is not only inevitable but a gracious gift from God.

The Gift of Suffering

How can suffering be a gift? The Greek word *charis* (grace, favour) underlies the phrase *"has been granted"* - suggesting that God's sovereign will includes suffering as part of the believer's journey. It is not a punishment or an accident; it's a divinely appointed privilege to suffer for Christ's sake. This calls to mind the paradox of the cross - that through suffering, Jesus accomplished our salvation.

Likewise, we are called to follow His footsteps, not only in joy and triumph but also in hardship. Suffering refines our faith like gold purified by fire (1 Peter 1:6-7). It exposes the idols of comfort and self-reliance in our hearts, driving us deeper into dependence on Christ. When we suffer for Him, our union with Him grows more intimate, and our faith becomes more genuine.

Consider the testimony of historical Christians like Dietrich Bonhoeffer, who embraced incredible suffering under Nazi persecution with great joy because he knew it was part of his witness for Christ. Or modern believers who face daily hardship yet radiate Christlike peace and courage. This kind of suffering cannot be mimicked by mere stoicism or resignation; it is supernatural, empowered by the Spirit.

Suffering as a Mark of True Discipleship

Jesus said, *"If anyone would come after me, let him deny himself and take up his cross daily and follow me."* (Luke 9:23). Suffering is thus a sign of true discipleship.

It distinguishes genuine followers of Christ from superficial believers or nominal Christians. The world may reject or persecute us, but that rejection confirms we belong to Christ.

Paul's reference to *"the same struggle you saw I had"* links the Philippians' suffering with his own. This shared experience creates a spiritual bond - they are united in the gospel through suffering. Suffering also serves as a witness to unbelievers. When they see Christians endure trials with grace, joy, and unwavering faith, it testifies to the transforming power of the gospel. It raises questions in their hearts: *"What is this hope that sustains them?"* This can open doors for gospel conversations.

Facing Suffering Today

How do we practically face suffering?

> ➢ **Recognize God's sovereignty:** Suffering is not random. It is part of God's redemptive plan to shape us and advance His kingdom.

> ➢ **Draw near to Christ:** Jesus is our compassionate High Priest who understands suffering intimately (Hebrews 4:15). He walks with us in every trial.

> ➢ **Support one another:** Like the Philippians and Paul, we are called to bear each other's burdens, pray for one another, and encourage steadfastness.

> ➢ **Rejoice always:** This is a most difficult command, but joy flows from the knowledge that suffering produces endurance, character, and hope (Romans 5:3-5).

> ➢ **Keep eternity in view:** Our present suffering is only temporary; our future glory is eternal. This hope fuels our perseverance.

Imagine a church where believers embrace suffering not with despair, but with joy - a church that stands firm under pressure, united in Spirit and purpose, shining brightly in a dark world. This is not idealistic; it is Paul's vision. The gospel transforms not only our beliefs but also our responses to hardship. It calls us to a courageous faith that declares: *"Even if I suffer, I belong to Christ, and this is for my good and His glory."* Are we ready to live that way? To welcome suffering as God's gift? To encourage one another in the struggle? To rejoice and stand firm, knowing our labour in the Lord is not in vain?

Conclusion: The Gospel and Our Suffering

Paul's closing words here wrap up a profound truth: Christian faith is inseparable from suffering. But that suffering is not a sign of failure - it is a sign of grace, calling, and community. As we face opposition, hardship, or loss, let us remember Paul's example and his encouragement to the Philippians.

Let us stand firm, strive together, and rejoice in the privilege of suffering for Christ. Because our lives are not our own. We belong to Him who suffered and died so that we might live - and in that, to live is truly Christ.

4. UNITING IN HUMILITY

Philippians 2:1-4 *"Therefore if you have any encouragement from being united with Christ, if any comfort from his love, if any common sharing in the Spirit, if any tenderness and compassion, then make my joy complete by being like-minded, having the same love, being one in spirit and of one mind. Do nothing out of selfish ambition or vain conceit. Rather, in humility value others above yourselves, not looking to your own interests but each of you to the interests of the others."*

The Motivation for Unity (2:1)

As we approach Philippians chapter 2, we reach one of the most profound and beautiful passages in the entire letter. The theme is unmistakable: unity through humility. In just four verses, Paul lays the foundation for what it means to live in a Christlike community.

The gospel, he says, not only reconciles us to God but also binds us to one another in love, tenderness, and shared purpose. But before Paul exhorts the Philippians on what they must do, he reminds them of what they already have. This is how grace works in the Christian life - it precedes obedience. Our actions flow not from obligation, but from identity. We live differently because we have been made new in Christ.

Verse 1 is a call to remember the blessings of salvation. *"Therefore, if you have any encouragement from being united with Christ, if any comfort from his love, if any common sharing in the Spirit, if any tenderness and compassion…"* Paul begins with the word *"Therefore,"* linking back to his earlier encouragement that believers should live *"in a manner worthy of the gospel"* (1:27), stand firm, strive together, and not fear suffering.

- 36 -

Now, building on that gospel-centred mindset, he turns their focus to the spiritual resources that empower their unity. Let's look closely at the four "*if*" statements Paul uses. These are not hypothetical "ifs" but rhetorical ones - they could easily be translated as "*since.*" Paul is not questioning whether these blessings exist; he is affirming them.

1. *"If you have any encouragement from being united with Christ..."*

The first motivation for unity is our encouragement in Christ. The Greek word used here (*paraklesis*) can mean comfort, consolation, or just support. Paul is pointing to the deep and sustaining encouragement that comes from being united with Jesus. This union with Christ is at the heart of our faith. We are not merely followers of Jesus - we are in Him. His death is our death, His resurrection is our resurrection, His righteousness is our righteousness.

That identity gives us hope when we're discouraged, strength when we're weak, and peace when we're anxious. Paul is saying, *"If you've ever been comforted by knowing Christ is with you and for you - then let that same spirit shape how you treat others."* The encouragement we receive from Christ should overflow in encouraging others.

2. *"If any comfort from his love..."*

Next, Paul appeals to the comfort that comes from Christ's love. This is the personal, tender, unwavering love that Christ has shown us. It is not abstract or distant - it is experienced. Have you ever been overwhelmed by the realization that Jesus loves you - not because of your performance, but in spite of it? Have you felt His presence during seasons of grief, failure, or loneliness? That comfort is real, and it anchors the soul.

Paul wants us to reflect: If you've been comforted by Jesus' love - then pass that comfort on. Be a source of healing and hope in your church. Don't sow discord or criticism - extend the same grace Christ has shown you.

3. "If any common sharing in the Spirit…"

The third motivation is fellowship with the Holy Spirit. The word "sharing" here is the Greek word *koinonia* - the deep, intimate fellowship that believers have through the indwelling Spirit of God. When we are saved, the Holy Spirit doesn't just visit us - He takes up residence in us. He binds us together as one body. He gives us unity not just of belief but of life. We are not a random collection of individuals; we are a Spirit-filled family.

This fellowship is not just vertical - between the believer and God - but horizontal, between believers themselves. The same Spirit who lives in you, lives in every other Christian. That shared life should lead to shared purpose, shared burdens, and shared joy. Paul's point is simple but profound: if you share in the life of the Spirit, then you must live in unity with those who share that same Spirit.

4. "If any tenderness and compassion…"

Paul appeals to the virtues of tenderness and compassion. These traits reflect the very heart of God. Jesus was moved with compassion for the crowds, for the sick, for the lost. He wept with those who wept. He touched the untouchable. He forgave the guilty. If we have received such mercy, should we not show it to others? If God has dealt gently with us, how can we be harsh, proud, or divisive?

These four blessings - encouragement in Christ, comfort from His love, fellowship in the Spirit, and God's tender mercy - form the motivation for unity.

Paul's message is: *"You have received so much from Christ - now let that overflow into your relationships with one another."*

Before we even get to Paul's command in verse 2, we must sit with these motivations. Ask yourself:

> ➤ Am I living daily in the encouragement of Christ, or do I let discouragement rule my spirit?
> ➤ Am I comforted by His love in a way that softens my approach to others?
> ➤ Do I recognize and honour the presence of the Spirit in fellow believers?
> ➤ Do I reflect Christ's tenderness and compassion in how I speak and act?

The Christian community cannot thrive on duty alone. It must be fuelled by grace - by a deep remembrance of what God has already done for us in Christ. That is the fuel for gospel-shaped unity.

The Call to Complete Unity (2:2)

"...then make my joy complete by being like-minded, having the same love, being one in spirit and of one mind." (Philippians 2:2) In verse 1, Paul reminds the Philippians of all they have received in Christ - encouragement, love, fellowship, and compassion.

Now, in verse 2, he turns the focus from what they've received to how they should respond. He is essentially saying, *"If you've experienced all of this grace from Christ, then this is how you should live in community with one another."*

Paul's heartfelt request is: *"Make my joy complete."* This is not a self-centred plea. Paul is not asking for attention or emotional gratification.

He's already rejoicing in what God has done among the Philippians, but he knows that their unity would bring his joy to its fullest expression. This reflects something powerful about the pastoral heart.

Paul's greatest joy is not in his own circumstances but in the spiritual health of the churches he loves. For Paul, the joy of seeing believers walking together in harmony - unified in Christ - outweighs even his own suffering in prison.

So how do they make his joy complete? Paul gives four expressions of unity that together form a picture of the kind of Christ-centred community every church should pursue.

1. "Being like-minded"

The phrase "like-minded" does not mean that everyone in the church must think exactly the same way about every issue. Paul is not calling for rigid conformity, but for spiritual alignment - a shared mindset centred on the gospel. The Greek literally means *"to think the same thing."* In other words, have the same spiritual outlook.

Have a gospel-centred worldview. Let the truth of Christ's life, death, and resurrection shape your priorities, your attitudes, and your goals. A church full of differing personalities, backgrounds, and opinions can still be unified when its people are united around the gospel.

So ask yourself: *Do I share the mind of Christ with my fellow believers? Do I see them not through the lens of preference or personality, but through the lens of grace?*

Being like-minded means that the mission of Christ matters more than our personal agendas. We yield our desires to the greater good of the church's calling. It's not about uniformity, but unity of purpose.

2. "Having the same love"

The second expression of unity is shared love. Paul says: *"Have the same love"* - the love that you have received from Christ, now extend that to one another. This is agape love - unconditional, self-giving, sacrificial love. It is not sentimental or surface-level. It is the kind of love that persists even when it's costly, even when people don't deserve it, even when emotions run dry.

Think of the example of Jesus washing His disciples' feet, including the one who would betray Him. Or His call to love our enemies and pray for those who persecute us. Christian love is rooted in divine grace, not human feeling. When every believer is committed to loving others the way Christ has loved them, unity naturally follows. Division often enters when we withhold love, when we become self-protective, or when we let bitterness take root.

To *"have the same love"* means that love must become the standard of how we treat everyone - not just those we like or agree with. It means loving the difficult person, the one who hurt us, the one who's different from us. Ask yourself: *Is there anyone in my church I'm struggling to love? How can I show them the same grace Christ has shown me?*

3. "Being one in spirit"

The third element of unity is being *"one in spirit."* Some translations say, *"being united in spirit,"* which captures the meaning well. Paul is speaking of inner harmony - a shared emotional connection, togetherness, and a strong sense of solidarity. This is not just theological agreement, but emotional unity. It's when believers truly care for one another, empathize with one another, and walk together through life's joys and trials. It's possible to agree on doctrine and still be cold or disconnected.

Paul wants something deeper: a church where hearts are knit together, where people weep with those who weep and rejoice with those who rejoice. This kind of unity is forged through prayer, vulnerability, service, and time spent together in Christ. It's what happens when people stop competing and start communing - when church becomes not just a place to attend, but a people to love.

4. "And of one mind"

Paul finishes the verse by repeating the call to unity in thinking: "and of one mind." Some translations render this as "intent on one purpose." The Greek suggests being "of one soul" - a deep, united focus on Christ's mission.

The church must have a shared direction. We are not just a gathering of individuals pursuing personal growth. We are a spiritual body, called to advance the gospel, glorify God, and build one another up.

Being "of one mind" means that we keep the main thing the main thing. We avoid distractions, petty divisions, or selfish ambitions that can derail the church's mission. This also means that leaders and members alike must prioritize unity. We must be willing to lay aside preferences, forgive offenses, and work through conflicts - not for the sake of peace alone, but for the sake of Christ's name.

When you look at Paul's vision in this verse - like-mindedness, shared love, spiritual harmony, and unified purpose - you begin to see what Christian community was meant to be. It's not a social club. It's not a consumer experience. It's a spirit-filled family, centred on Christ, marked by love, and moving together in mission.

Such unity is not automatic. It must be pursued, protected, and preserved. It requires humility, patience, and sacrifice.

But when we live this way, the church then becomes a compelling witness to the world. Jesus said, *"By this everyone will know that you are my disciples, if you love one another."* (John 13:35).

So let us examine our hearts:

> ➤ Am I contributing to the unity of my church or undermining it?
> ➤ Do I value Christ's mission more than my own preferences?
> ➤ Am I willing to love sacrificially, even when it's hard?
> ➤ Am I walking in step with my brothers and sisters - or pulling away?

Paul says, *"Make my joy complete."* But it's not just his joy at stake. It is the joy of Christ when His people live in the unity His Spirit has made possible.

The Path to Unity - Humility in Action (2:3-4)

"Do nothing out of selfish ambition or vain conceit. Rather, in humility value others above yourselves, not looking to your own interests but each of you to the interests of the others." (Philippians 2:3-4). In this final portion of Philippians 2:1-4, Paul moves from the call to unity into the essential attitude that sustains it: humility. If unity is the goal, then humility is the road that gets us there.

Paul knows the human heart. He understands how easily pride, competition, and self-centeredness can disrupt fellowship, even among mature Christians. So he speaks directly to the motives that undermine unity and points us to the heart posture that reflects Christ Himself. Let's unpack his command piece by piece and allow the Spirit to examine our hearts.

1. "Do nothing out of selfish ambition or vain conceit"

Here Paul addresses two dangerous attitudes that tear communities apart: selfish ambition and vain conceit. Selfish ambition refers to a self-seeking spirit - the desire to promote oneself, to gain recognition, to push one's agenda regardless of the cost to others. It's a competitive mindset that treats church life like a platform or a contest.

This was the spirit of the world in Paul's day, and it is no less present today. In fact, Paul already mentioned selfish ambition earlier in this letter (Philippians 1:17), criticizing those who preached Christ *"out of selfish ambition, not sincerely."* Even gospel ministry, if corrupted by pride, can become a platform for self.

Vain conceit (or "empty glory") is another form of pride. It's the internal belief that we are more important than we are. It seeks praise, entitlement, or superiority - all of which are rooted in a hunger for glory that belongs to God alone. Paul says clearly: *Do nothing* - not a single word, decision, or action - from these motives. This is not a call to low self-esteem, but to right-sized self-awareness. The gospel reminds us that apart from Christ, we are nothing - and in Christ, we are everything because of Him, not because of ourselves. That truth frees us from chasing approval and allows us to serve joyfully and sincerely.

2. "Rather, in humility value others above yourselves"

The antidote to selfishness and pride is humility. In the Roman world, humility was not seen as a virtue. It was associated with weakness, shame, and servitude. But in the gospel, humility becomes the mark of greatness. Jesus Himself redefined greatness by washing His disciples' feet and laying down His life. And Paul says: *This must be your posture too.*

To *"value others above yourselves"* doesn't mean denying your worth or hating yourself. It really means consciously choosing to elevate others - their needs, their preferences, their stories - above your own. It's actually the opposite of entitlement. It's the opposite of always needing to be right, or in control, or at the centre.

Humility begins with the recognition that every person you meet is someone for whom Christ died. If the Son of God found them worthy of His blood, how can we not treat them with dignity and care?

Imagine what would happen in your church, your family, your workplace, if every believer began to truly value others above themselves. The conflicts would decrease. Compassion would increase. Competition would give way to cooperation. But this kind of humility isn't natural. It requires a daily decision to die to self and live for Christ.

3. *"Not looking to your own interests but each of you to the interests of the others"*

Paul takes humility further here. It's not just a mindset - it's a lifestyle. Humility is always expressed through practical concern for others. To *"look to the interests of others"* means to consider their needs, desires, and struggles as if they were your own. It's not about ignoring your own responsibilities or needs - but about expanding your focus beyond yourself.

We live in a culture that constantly tells us to *"look out for number one."* But the gospel calls us to a better way - to look out for one another, to carry each other's burdens, to rejoice and weep together. Paul does not say this is the role of a few special Christians. He says, *"each of you"* - every believer is called to this way of living. This kind of love is deeply relational.

It requires us to know one another - to listen, to observe, to be present. We can't look out for someone's interests if we are too busy with our own lives to notice them. This is what transforms a congregation from being a crowd of individuals to being a family - a gospel-shaped, Spirit-filled family where people are deeply committed to one another's flourishing. How can we begin to cultivate this kind of humility? Here are some spiritual disciplines and heart checks that can help:

➢ *Start with the gospel every day:* Remind yourself that you are saved by grace, not by performance. That truth levels all pride and raises the lowly.

➢ *Pray for others regularly:* Interceding for others softens your heart and expands your perspective. *Listen more than you speak:* Listening is one of the most practical ways to value others above yourself.

➢ *Serve in hidden ways:* Do things that no one will see or applaud - and do them joyfully. This trains your heart away from *"vain conceit."*

➢ *Celebrate others' successes:* When someone else is honoured or blessed, rejoice with them without envy.

➢ *Apologize quickly:* When you've hurt someone, own it. Humility repents without defensiveness. *Practice gratitude:* A grateful heart is a humble heart which acknowledges that every good thing is from God.

When these practices take root, humility stops being a theory and becomes a way of life.

Conclusion

Paul's vision in Philippians 2:1-4 is not just about individual behaviour. It's actually about creating a whole community that reflects Jesus.

A people who are united, joyful, selfless, and humble. A church that looks so different from the world that people take notice and ask, *"What is this hope you have? Who is this Christ you follow?"*

This passage sets the stage for the next verses, where Paul will describe Christ's humility in going to the cross. But here, he's showing us that before we marvel at Christ's humility, we must be ready to mirror it. Unity and humility go hand in hand. One cannot exist without the other. And both are possible only through the gospel - through the transforming power of Jesus Christ who laid down His life for us.

So let us be a people who do nothing out of selfish ambition, who daily choose to value others, who look out for the interests of those around us - and who, in doing so, show the world what it means to follow Christ.

5. THE MIND OF CHRIST

Philippians 2:5-11 *"In your relationships with one another, have the same mindset as Christ Jesus: Who, being in very nature God, did not consider equality with God something to be used to his own advantage; rather, he made himself nothing by taking the very nature of a servant, being made in human likeness. And being found in appearance as a man, he humbled himself by becoming obedient to death - even death on a cross!*

Therefore God exalted him to the highest place and gave him the name that is above every name, that at the name of Jesus every knee should bow, in heaven and on earth and under the earth, and every tongue acknowledge that Jesus Christ is Lord, to the glory of God the Father."

Cultivating the Mindset of Christ (2:5)

"In your relationships with one another, have the same mindset as Christ Jesus..." (Philippians 2:5). With this verse, Paul transitions from exhortation to example. Having just called the Philippians to unity and humility in their relationships (Philippians 2:1-4), he now points them to the ultimate model: Jesus Christ Himself.

This verse is both a bridge and a command. It bridges the call to humility in verses 1-4 with the glorious Christ hymn in verses 6-11. And it issues a command that touches the very core of Christian discipleship: *"Have the same mindset as Christ Jesus."* This is not a call to imitate Jesus from a distance. It is a summons to let the very thoughts, values, and attitudes of Jesus shape every part of our lives. The word *"mindset"* (*phroneō*) refers not merely to thoughts but to a whole orientation of the heart - the way we perceive ourselves, others, and God. So what does it mean to have the mind of Christ?

Let's explore three key truths from this short but weighty verse.

1. The Mind of Christ is Relational

Notice Paul's emphasis: *"In your relationships with one another..."* This mindset is not developed in isolation. It is forged in the fire of community - through real, sometimes difficult, relationships within the body of Christ. Christian maturity is not merely shown by private devotion but by public humility - especially in how we treat others.

It's easy to imagine ourselves as Christlike when we're alone with our Bibles open. But the test comes when we're wronged, overlooked, misunderstood, or perhaps asked to serve in inconvenient ways.

To *"have the same mindset as Christ Jesus"* is to see every relationship as an opportunity to reflect Christ - not to win arguments or assert superiority, but to embody His grace, humility, and love. Ask yourself: *What is my mindset when I'm interrupted? When someone disagrees with me? When I feel entitled to be served but am instead asked to serve?* The mind of Christ is not selfish. It is not reactive. It is deliberately oriented toward others in love - and especially so when that love costs something.

2. The Mind of Christ Is Self-Emptying

While verse 5 doesn't yet describe what Jesus did, it sets the tone for what follows. The verses immediately after (vv. 6-8) describe Christ's astonishing humility - His willingness to lay aside divine privilege, take on human form, and obey even unto death. Paul is preparing us: *This is the mindset you are called to emulate.* A mindset that says, "*I will not cling to my rights. I will not insist on my position. I will lower myself to lift others up."*

This was revolutionary in Paul's day - and it still is now. The world tells us to protect ourselves, to promote ourselves, to prioritize our comfort. But Christ's example calls us to the opposite: to surrender status and serve in love. This mindset is not about thinking less of yourself but thinking of yourself less. It is a posture of the heart that says: *"How can I serve? Whom can I bless? What might it cost me to love like Jesus?"*

And let's be honest: this is not easy. Humility grates against our flesh. We want to be noticed, appreciated, and admired. But the more we gaze at Christ and are filled with His Spirit, the more we are transformed into His image - and the more natural it becomes to serve without being seen, to forgive without being asked, to sacrifice without recognition.

3. The Mind of Christ is Already Yours in Christ

This verse is a command, but it's also a reminder of your identity. Paul is not saying, *"Try really hard to think like Jesus."* He is saying, *"Live out what is already yours because you are in Christ."* As believers, we are united with Christ. His Spirit dwells in us.

We don't merely admire Jesus from afar - we are empowered by His presence within us. The mind of Christ is not a lofty ideal for the spiritual elite. It is the daily calling of every Christian - and by God's grace, it is possible.

In 1 Corinthians 2:16 we read, *"But we have the mind of Christ."* Not *we might have*, or *we will one day have*, but *we have*. That's the miracle of the gospel. Christ not only saves us - He transforms us from the inside out. So the call to have His mindset is not a burden but a gift. It's a call to live in line with your new nature - to become, in practice, who you already are in position.

How can we grow in this mindset? Consider these three spiritual disciplines:

➢ *Meditate on Christ's humility:* Regularly read and reflect on Philippians 2:6-8. Let the image of the self-emptying Savior shape how you think about leadership, sacrifice, and love.

➢ *Practice humility in hidden ways:* Look for small, unseen opportunities to serve others. Let go of the need for recognition. Ask God to purify your motives.

➢ *Invite the Spirit to renew your mind:* Spend time in prayer asking the Holy Spirit to transform your thoughts, priorities, and responses. Let Him root out pride and cultivate Christlike attitudes.

Verse 5 is a pivot point in Philippians. It invites us to look beyond ourselves and up to Christ. It challenges us to reimagine greatness, to embrace humility, and to love sacrificially. This is not an abstract principle. It is the very heartbeat of Christian discipleship: *to be conformed to the image of the Son.* And that begins with the way we think - with the mindset we carry into every conversation, every decision, and every relationship.

So let us ask today: *Do I have the mind of Christ? And if not, am I willing to ask God to cultivate it in me - for the sake of His glory and the good of His church?*

Christ's Descent into Humility (2:6–8)

Having issued the command in verse 5 to have the same mindset as Christ Jesus, Paul now unveils the stunning model of that mindset in verses 6-8. These verses are among the most sacred in all Scripture – they are often referred to as the *Christ Hymn* - and they contain some of the richest Christology in the New Testament.

They outline a descent so deep, so gracious, so sacrificial, that it humbles every heart that beholds it. In the previous section we learned that the Christian life requires us to cultivate the mindset of Christ. Now Paul shows us what that mindset looks like in action - and it begins with the unimaginable: the eternal Son of God making Himself nothing for us.

Christ's Pre-existence and Divine Nature (v. 6)

"Who, being in very nature God, did not consider equality with God something to be used to his own advantage..." Paul begins by affirming that Jesus, before His incarnation, already existed in the *"very nature"* of God. The Greek word used here is *morphē*, which speaks of essence or essential being. This is not a suggestion that Jesus was merely godlike - it is an emphatic statement that Jesus is fully and eternally God.

He shared all the attributes of divinity: power, glory, omniscience, and holiness. He existed from eternity past, co-equal with the Father and the Spirit. And yet - and this is the wonder - He did not consider this equality something to cling to or exploit for His own gain.

The phrase *"something to be used to his own advantage"* could also be rendered *"something to be grasped."* It carries the sense of seizing or holding onto a privilege. Jesus did not exploit His divine status. He did not clutch His heavenly rights with tight fists. Instead, He opened His hands - and emptied Himself.

This is the beginning of His humility: not a loss of divinity, but a refusal to use His divinity as a tool for self-preservation. How different this is from how we act when we have power. We so often protect it, guard it, assert it. But Jesus relinquished it - not His divine nature, but His divine privilege.

2. Christ's Self-Emptying and Servanthood (v. 7)

"...rather, he made himself nothing by taking the very nature of a servant, being made in human likeness." Here is one of the most astounding phrases in all of Scripture: *"He made himself nothing."* Some translations say, *"He emptied himself."* Again, this doesn't mean that Christ stopped being God - rather, He voluntarily laid aside His rights, privileges, and heavenly glory. He took on all the limitations and all the vulnerabilities of a human life.

How did Jesus empty Himself? He did so by taking something, not by *losing* something: *"by taking the very nature of a servant."* There is a beautiful irony here. Christ, who is in the form of God, takes the form (*morphē*) of a servant - the same word used for *"very nature."* He doesn't just look like a servant; He becomes one in essence and action. This is not a divine being disguising Himself temporarily. This is God embracing servanthood in its fullness. Jesus didn't just do servant-like things - He became a servant.

Paul continues: He was *"made in human likeness."* The eternal Son of God took on a real human body, real human limitations, real human emotions, and real human experiences. He slept, wept, walked, grew tired, and felt hunger. He entered the full reality of humanity - all without sin. This is the miracle of the incarnation: God became man, not to be served, but to serve. In a world obsessed with climbing higher, Jesus descended lower.

3. Christ's Humble Obedience to Death (v. 8)

"And being found in appearance as a man, he humbled himself by becoming obedient to death - even death on a cross!" Here, Paul completes the descent. Not only did Christ take on flesh, not only did He live as a servant - He humbled Himself to the point of death.

Notice the choice: *"He humbled himself."* No one humbled Him. No one forced Him into suffering. He chose it. This was a voluntary act of obedience and love. Obedience is central here: *"obedient to death." This* recalls the Garden of Gethsemane, where Jesus prayed, *"Not my will, but yours be done."* He obeyed the Father's will even when it led Him to agony, shame, and crucifixion. And Paul adds one more shocking detail: *"even death on a cross."* This is not just death - it is the most humiliating, excruciating, and shameful form of execution known in the ancient world. Crucifixion was reserved for criminals and slaves. It was designed to maximize pain and disgrace.

For a Jew, it was especially offensive - for Scripture says, *"Cursed is everyone who hangs on a tree"* (Galatians 3:13). And yet this is the very path Jesus chose. Think about that: the eternal Son of God submitted not only to death, but to the most degrading death imaginable.

Why? Because our salvation depended on it. Because only by bearing our curse, our shame, our punishment, could He redeem us. This is the climax of humility. Christ didn't just stoop low - He went all the way to the bottom, so that He might lift us up.

Paul shows us the descent of Christ not simply to amaze us - though it surely should - but to inspire and empower us to imitate it.

- ➢ When we are tempted to cling to our individual rights, we remember that Jesus relinquished His.

- ➢ When we are reluctant to serve, we remember that Jesus became a servant.

- ➢ When we resist humility, we remember that Jesus humbled Himself all the way to the cross.

This is the mindset we are called to embrace - not because it's easy or natural, but because it is Christlike. It's only when we embrace the downward path of humility that we are prepared to experience the upward call of exaltation - which is where Paul will take us next in verses 9-11.

The Exaltation of Christ (2:9–11)

Having traced Christ's breathtaking descent in verses 6-8, from heavenly glory to human servanthood, all the way to death on a cross - Paul now declares the glorious result: Christ's exaltation. This is the Father's response to the Son's humble obedience.

It is the great reversal of the gospel: the way down is the way up. In these verses, Paul declares that Jesus has been lifted to the highest possible place and given the name that commands worship throughout the entire cosmos. But notice how it begins: with the word "therefore."

1. God's Response to Humility Is Exaltation

"Therefore God exalted him to the highest place..." Christ's exaltation is the direct result of His self-emptying obedience. He humbled Himself - *therefore* God lifted Him up. This pattern is woven throughout Scripture. Proverbs 18:12 says, *"Humility comes before honour."* James 4:10 urges us, *"Humble yourselves before the Lord, and he will lift you up."* Jesus Himself said, *"Whoever exalts himself will be humbled, and whoever humbles himself will be exalted."* (Matthew 23:12).

And no one humbled Himself more than Jesus - so no one has been exalted more than Jesus. This exaltation is not simply a return to where Christ began. It is a glorified affirmation of who He is - the *crucified* and *risen* Lord. The One who bore the cross is now crowned with glory.

The phrase *"exalted to the highest place"* is one word in Greek: *hyperupsōsen* – with the meaning: *"super-exalted"* or *"highly exalted beyond measure."* Christ has been lifted to the supreme place of honour, authority, and majesty. This reminds us that in God's kingdom, true greatness comes through humble obedience. The world prizes power and pride; God honours humility and sacrifice.

2. The Name Above Every Name

"...and gave him the name that is above every name..." What is this name that God has given to Jesus? It may seem at first that the name is "Jesus" - but Paul has already used that name in earlier verses.

The key comes in verse 11: *"Jesus Christ is Lord."* The name that is above every name is "Lord." In the Greek Old Testament (the Septuagint), *"Lord"* (*Kyrios*) was the translation of the divine name *Yahweh*.

To say *"Jesus is Lord"* is to declare that Jesus shares the divine identity. He is not merely a great teacher or prophet - He is God, worthy of worship, obedience, and allegiance. This was a radical confession in Paul's day. In the Roman Empire, Caesar was hailed as *"Lord."* To say *"Jesus is Lord"* was not only a theological statement - but it was also a political act of courage and loyalty to a greater King.

And it still is today. In a world full of competing authorities, ideologies, and allegiances, Christians declare: *Jesus alone is Lord.* Not success. Not comfort. Not fame. Not country. Not self. Jesus is Lord.

And this name - this Lordship - is above every other name. There is no rival to His throne. No competitor for His glory. No other name by which we are saved (Acts 4:12).

3. Universal Worship and Acknowledgment

"... that at the name of Jesus every knee should bow, in heaven and on earth and under the earth, and every tongue acknowledge that Jesus Christ is Lord..." Paul now envisions the universal recognition of Christ's Lordship. This is not optional or partial - it is total and inevitable. Every creature, in every realm, will bow before Jesus.

> ➤ *"In heaven"* - the angels and redeemed saints.
> ➤ *"On earth"* - every human being living today.
> ➤ *"Under the earth"* - even the realm of the dead and the demonic.

This is a sweeping, cosmic vision of worship. One day, every knee will bow - either willingly in joyful adoration, or unwillingly in final submission. One day, every tongue will confess - either now, in saving faith, or later, in judgment. This should stir both hope and urgency in us. Hope - because Jesus will be vindicated, and justice will prevail. Urgency - because now is the time of grace. Now is the day to bow the knee willingly, to confess with joy that *Jesus Christ is Lord.*

This passage also shapes our present worship. When we gather as a church, we are joining a foretaste of this eternal reality. Every time we sing, serve, give, pray, and declare Jesus as Lord, we are aligning ourselves with the future - when heaven and earth will be united in His praise.

4. All to the Glory of God the Father

"...to the glory of God the Father." Finally, Paul concludes with the ultimate purpose of Christ's exaltation: the glory of God the Father. Even in His exaltation, Jesus does not seek independent glory. As He always did on earth, He brings glory to His Father.

There is no competition in the Trinity - only perfect harmony. The Son glorifies the Father. The Father exalts the Son. The Spirit magnifies them both. And we are invited into this divine joy - not to seek our own glory, but to live for the glory of God.

This is the purpose of your salvation. This is the purpose of Christ's coming. This is the reason you exist: *to glorify God and enjoy Him forever.* So when we bow to Jesus, when we confess Him as Lord, when we adopt His mindset of humility - God is glorified.

What does this final movement of the Christ hymn mean for our daily lives?

1. *Worship with awe and reverence*: Jesus is not just your friend - He is Lord of all. Approach Him with joyful reverence. Let your heart be full of wonder at who He is and what He has done.

2. *Live in submission to Christ's authority*: If Jesus is Lord, then His Word is final. His commands are not suggestions. Obedience is not optional. Submit every area of your life - your time, relationships, finances, and desires - to His Lordship.

3. *Proclaim Christ boldly*: Every tongue will one day confess - but now is the time for the church to declare it loudly and clearly. Let your life and lips point others to the exalted Christ.

4. *Hope in His ultimate victory*: In a world of chaos, injustice, and rebellion, remember: the risen Christ is on the throne. He will return. He will reign. And every knee will bow.

Conclusion

Philippians 2:5-11 has taken us on a journey:

> ➤ From Christ's divine glory...

> ➤ To His self-emptying humility...

> ➤ To His obedient death...

> ➤ To His triumphant exaltation.

This is the pattern of the gospel: *glory to humility to greater glory.* And it is the pattern for every believer. If we humble ourselves, if we take up our cross and follow Jesus, we too will share in His glory.

So let us embrace the mind of Christ - in our homes, our churches, our communities. Let us go low, so that God may lift us up. Let us worship the One who stooped to save us - and who now reigns forever as Lord of all.

To Him be the glory, now and forever. Amen.

6. SHINE AS LIGHTS IN THE DARKNESS

Philippians 2:12-18 *"Therefore, my dear friends, as you have always obeyed - not only in my presence, but now much more in my absence - continue to work out your salvation with fear and trembling, for it is God who works in you to will and to act in order to fulfill his good purpose.*

Do everything without grumbling or arguing, so that you may become blameless and pure, "children of God without fault in a warped and crooked generation." Then you will shine among them like stars in the sky as you hold firmly to the word of life. And then I will be able to boast on the day of Christ that I did not run or labour in vain.

But even if I am being poured out like a drink offering on the sacrifice and service coming from your faith, I am glad and rejoice with all of you. So you too should be glad and rejoice with me."

Living Out Our Salvation (Philippians 2:12–13)

As Paul continues his letter, he transitions from the exaltation of Christ in verses 9–11 to the application of that truth in the believer's daily life.

"Therefore, my dear friends, as you have always obeyed - not only in my presence, but now much more in my absence - continue to work out your salvation with fear and trembling, for it is God who works in you to will and to act in order to fulfill his good purpose." (Philippians 2:12–13)

In light of Christ's example of humility and obedience, we are now called to live out our salvation — not to earn it, but to embody it. These two verses are rich in meaning and often misunderstood, so let's explore them carefully.

1. Obedience is the Natural Fruit of Salvation

Paul begins affectionately, addressing the Philippians as *"my dear friends,"* or more literally, *"my beloved."* This is not the tone of a cold theologian - it's the heart of a spiritual father who delights in his children's growth. He commends them for their consistent obedience - both when he was with them and now in his absence. This points to the sincerity of their faith. Obedience is not meant to be seasonal or dependent on external pressure. The true test of maturity is how we walk when no one is watching.

Paul then gives this command: *"Continue to work out your salvation with fear and trembling."* This is one of the most debated verses in Philippians, and it's crucial we understand what Paul is saying - and what he is not saying. He is not saying, *"Work* for *your salvation."* Salvation is a gift of grace, not a result of human effort (Ephesians 2:8-9).

Paul has already made this clear in all his writings. Instead, he says, *"Work* out *your salvation."* That is, live out what God has already worked in. The Greek word for *"work out"* (*katergazesthe*) means to carry something to completion, to bring it to full expression. It's the idea of mining out the richness of what you've been given. You already possess salvation in Christ - now develop it, express it, and live it out in every area of life.

2. With Fear and Trembling - Why?

Paul adds that this working out should be done *"with fear and trembling."* That may strike us as odd. Aren't we supposed to rejoice in our salvation? Absolutely - but joy and reverence are not enemies. In fact, they often go together in Scripture. The *"fear of the Lord"* is not cringing terror - it's a deep, awe-filled reverence for God. It's the sense of His holiness, His majesty, and His presence.

When we understand who God is - and what He has done to save us - we don't treat our salvation casually. We don't reduce discipleship to hobbies or preferences. We approach our daily walk with a serious desire to honour the One who bought us with His blood.

This reverent attitude guards us from two dangerous extremes: pride ("I've got this on my own") and laziness ("God will just do it for me"). Instead, we are to walk in humble obedience, empowered by grace, motivated by awe.

3. God Is the One Who Works in You

Now, lest we misunderstand and think it's all up to us, Paul adds one of the most liberating truths in Scripture: *"For it is God who works in you to will and to act in order to fulfill his good purpose."* What a relief. Yes, we are called to work out our salvation - but only because God is already at work within us. This verse balances the tension between divine sovereignty and human responsibility. We act, we obey, we grow - but only because God is energizing us from within.

The Greek word for "works" is *energeō* - the root of our word *"energy."* God supplies the power. He gives both the desire ("to will") and the ability ("to act"). That means every time we hunger for holiness, every time we choose righteousness, every time we persevere through trial - it is God working in us.

This should fill us with both comfort and confidence. We're not alone in our Christian walk. We're not left to figure it out by ourselves. The same God who saved us is now shaping us - from the inside out - for His good purpose. And what is His good purpose? Ultimately, to conform us to the image of His Son (Romans 8:29), and to glorify His name through our transformed lives.

So what does this mean for us today?

- ➢ If you are in Christ, your salvation is secure. But it's not static. You are called to grow, to obey, in reverence.
- ➢ Don't treat your spiritual life lightly. Approach it with seriousness - not in fear of condemnation, but in awe of grace.
- ➢ Remember, your efforts are not your own. God is working in you. You are not striving alone. His power is at work in your will and actions.

Paul will go on in the next verses to show what this kind of life looks like in a dark world. But it all begins here: with a life that is grounded in salvation, fuelled by grace, and motivated by reverent joy.

Shining in a Crooked and Depraved Generation (2:14–16)

In Part 1, we examined Paul's challenge to work out our salvation with fear and trembling, grounded in the assurance that God is powerfully at work within us. Now in verses 14-16, Paul moves from that foundational principle to a very practical expression of gospel living. If God is at work in us, if we are truly His redeemed people, then our lives should visibly reflect His light - especially in a world full of darkness.

Let's read this next section carefully: *"Do everything without grumbling or arguing, so that you may become blameless and pure, 'children of God without fault in a warped and crooked generation.' Then you will shine among them like stars in the sky as you hold firmly to the word of life."* (2:14–16a).

This passage calls the church to live in such a radically different way that the world sees Christ in us - not just in our doctrine or words, but in our very attitudes and behaviours.

1. A Call to Radical Attitudes (v.14)

"Do everything without grumbling or arguing..." Paul begins with this specific command: *"Do everything without grumbling or arguing."* Why focus on this? Why, after such high theological truths about Christ's humility and God's working in us, does Paul zero in on *grumbling*? The answer is simple: nothing undermines Christian witness more quickly than a complaining or divisive spirit. We may affirm great truths with our lips, but if our hearts are full of bitterness, if our mouths are constantly critical or contentious, our testimony collapses.

This word *"grumbling"* (Greek: *goggysmos*) reminds us of the murmurings of the Israelites in the wilderness - a repeated failure to trust in God's provision and leadership. Despite God's many miracles, the Israelites grumbled about food, water, leadership, and danger. They failed to believe that God was both sovereign and good - and that posture of discontentment led to disobedience and discipline.

"Arguing" (*dialogismos*) points to disputes and divisiveness - the kind of constant debating or contention that fractures community and hinders gospel unity. When the church is consumed with internal strife, it becomes distracted from its mission and distorted in its witness. Paul is not suggesting that every believer must always feel cheerful - he knows suffering and sorrow are real. But he is urging us to adopt a spirit of trusting contentment and relational unity, even when circumstances are difficult. This is part of working out our salvation: our attitudes and actions matter.

2. Becoming Blameless and Pure (v.15a)

"...so that you may become blameless and pure, children of God without fault..." The purpose behind this command now becomes clearer.

By rejecting a complaining or argumentative spirit, we position ourselves to grow into the character God desires for His children. The terms *"blameless"* and *"pure"* are closely linked. *"Blameless"* refers to being above reproach - not giving the world just cause to accuse us of hypocrisy or sin. *"Pure"* refers to sincerity and integrity - being the same in private as in public, without hidden motives or deception.

Paul isn't describing sinless perfection, but spiritual maturity. As we walk in obedience and reverence, God shapes us to become more like His Son - authentic, trustworthy, holy witnesses in a fallen world.

He adds that we are *"children of God without fault,"* echoing the identity bestowed on us through Christ. We are not trying to earn God's approval; we are living in a way that reflects who we already are: adopted sons and daughters of a holy God. That identity should shape our behaviour. The more we reflect our Father's character, the more clearly the world sees Him through us.

3. Living in a Warped and Crooked Generation (v.15b)

"...in a warped and crooked generation." This phrase is drawn directly from Deuteronomy 32:5, where Moses rebukes Israel for their unfaithfulness. Paul uses it here to describe the moral and spiritual condition of the unbelieving world. The words *"warped"* and *"crooked"* paint a picture of distortion - what God created to be upright and good has been bent out of shape by sin. This is not a new phenomenon.

Every generation, in every culture, has been marred by rebellion against God. But what matters most is what Paul says next. In this dark world, he doesn't call Christians to retreat or despair. He calls us to shine.

4. Shining Like Stars in the Sky (v.15c)

"Then you will shine among them like stars in the sky..." Here is one of the most beautiful images in all of Paul's letters. In the midst of a dark and broken world, the people of God are called to shine like stars - or more literally, *luminaries*.

Think of the stars. In the vast blackness of night, their light is unmistakable. Even a single star catches the eye because of the contrast with its surroundings. The darker the sky, the brighter the stars appear.

This is Paul's vision for the church. He's not calling for popularity, power, or prestige. He's calling for contrast. In a world of grumbling, we give thanks. In a culture of division, we show unity. In the midst of despair, we live with hope. That is how we shine.

And notice: we shine *"among them."* This is not a call to escape the world, but to live differently *in the midst* of it. Jesus said the same in Matthew 5:14-16 - *"You are the light of the world... let your light shine before others."* We are not called to hide our faith, but to display it humbly and boldly.

The early church changed the Roman Empire not through military might or cultural dominance, but through the radiant witness of faithful lives - people who loved their enemies, cared for the sick, valued the poor, and suffered with joy. That's the kind of light that changes the world.

5. Holding Firmly to the Word of Life (v.16a)

"...as you hold firmly to the word of life." How do we shine like this? Paul tells us: by holding firmly to the word of life. The *"word of life"* is the gospel - the message of salvation through Christ, revealed in Scripture. It is both the message we proclaim and the truth we build our lives upon.

The phrase *"hold firmly"* can also be translated *"hold fast"* or even *"hold out."* Both meanings apply: *Hold fast:* cling to God's Word in faith, refusing to be swayed by error, compromise, or cultural pressure.

Scripture is our source of truth, identity, and strength. *Hold out:* offer the gospel to others.

The light we shine is not our own; it's the light of Christ, and we are called to extend it to a dying world. If we drift from God's Word, our light dims. But if we root ourselves in it, we remain bright beacons of grace and truth.

Let's summarize the challenge of this passage for our lives today:

➢ *Guard your attitude:* Grumbling and arguing may seem like small sins, but they have a corrosive effect on your soul and your witness. Cultivate a spirit of gratitude and peace.

➢ *Pursue character:* Strive to be blameless and pure - not to earn God's love, but to reflect it. Let the world see what it means to be a child of God.

➢ *Engage the world without becoming like it:* We are called to shine in the darkness - not blend into it. Let your life be marked by contrast, not conformity.

➢ *Stay anchored in the Word:* The gospel is your power source. Let it shape your mind, fuel your obedience, and guide your mission.

➢ *Shine together:* Paul writes this to a community, not individuals alone. The church shines brightest when it shines together - united in love, rooted in truth, committed to the mission.

Rejoicing in Sacrifice (2:16b–18)

"And then I will be able to boast on the day of Christ that I did not run or labour in vain. But even if I am being poured out like a drink offering on the sacrifice and service coming from your faith, I am glad and rejoice with all of you. So you too should be glad and rejoice with me."

After calling the Philippians to live out their salvation and shine like stars in a dark world, Paul now reflects on his own ministry, his potential sacrifice, and the eternal joy that comes from a life fully surrendered to Christ. This is a deeply personal and profoundly pastoral section of the letter, where Paul pulls back the curtain to show how he views both his suffering and theirs in light of eternity.

1. A Life That Is Not Wasted (v.16b)

"And then I will be able to boast on the day of Christ that I did not run or labour in vain." Paul longs for one thing above all else: that his ministry will be fruitful and enduring in the lives of those he served. He pictures the *"day of Christ"* - that final day when Jesus returns, when all will be revealed and judged in righteousness. His desire is to be able to look back and rejoice, not regret - to know that his work among the Philippians was not wasted, not empty, not *"in vain."* The metaphors he uses here - *"run"* and *"labour"* – both convey exertion, effort, and intentional sacrifice. Paul gave his life for the gospel, and he wants to know that it counted.

This longing speaks to every pastor, every leader, every disciple-maker. We pour into people's lives - sometimes with joy, sometimes with tears. We teach, we pray, we serve, we correct. And deep down we wonder: Will it last? Will it bear fruit? Paul teaches us that eternal joy comes from seeing others stand firm in Christ - not because it glorifies us, but because it glorifies God.

Our greatest reward is not recognition in this life, but celebration in the next - when we see lives transformed by the gospel we proclaimed and modelled. It also challenges every believer: Are we living in a way that validates the labour of those who discipled us? Are we pressing on in the faith, holding fast to the Word, and shining brightly - or have we drifted? One of the greatest encouragements we can give to our leaders is to stay faithful to Christ.

2. A Life Willingly Poured Out (v.17)

"But even if I am being poured out like a drink offering on the sacrifice and service coming from your faith..." Here, Paul gives us one of the most vivid and moving pictures in the New Testament - the image of a life poured out in worship. In the Old Testament sacrificial system, a drink offering was often added to a burnt offering or grain offering.

It was a final act of dedication, where wine was poured out at the altar, symbolizing complete surrender and devotion to God (see Exodus 29:40-41, Numbers 15:1–10). Paul applies this to himself. He sees his life - and perhaps even his impending death - as a drink offering to be poured out. It is not the main sacrifice (that is the Philippians' faith and service), but it is poured out alongside theirs. What a powerful image of partnership! Paul doesn't exalt himself; he says, *"Your faith and service are the real offering - I'm just the wine poured beside it."*

This is the essence of Christian ministry - not seeking centre stage but joyfully offering oneself in support of others. Paul's entire life, and possibly even his death, was offered to God for the growth and perseverance of the church. And here is the remarkable part: he rejoices. *"I am glad and rejoice with all of you."* Paul is not bitter. He doesn't complain. He doesn't see his suffering as a tragedy or waste. He sees it as worship.

Even if he never gets out of prison, even if his life ends in martyrdom, it's worth it - because God is glorified and the church is growing.

This challenges our modern mindset profoundly. We often ask, *"What will I get from this?"* or *"Is this worth my time?"* But Paul asks, *"Is this honouring to Christ?"* and *"Does this strengthen His people?"*

To live this way, we must surrender our comfort, our control, and our craving for recognition. We must view our lives as instruments of worship - to be poured out, not stored up. The value of our life is not in how much we preserve it, but in how faithfully we spend it for the gospel.

3. A Joy that is Shared (v.18)

"So you too should be glad and rejoice with me." Paul refuses to make his sacrifice a source of sorrow. Instead, he invites the Philippians to rejoice with him. In other words, *"Don't feel sorry for me - join me in joy."* This is not denial or toxic positivity; it's gospel perspective. Paul sees everything - even suffering - through the lens of eternity. He knows that when the church is faithful, when lives are transformed, when Christ is exalted, then even sacrifice is reason for celebration. And he wants the church to see it too. Rejoicing is not reserved for easy times. True gospel joy transcends circumstances. It is not rooted in how things feel, but in what God is doing.

This kind of joy is contagious. When leaders rejoice in the midst of trials, the church is strengthened. When we celebrate what God is doing - even in difficulty - our faith becomes resilient. Joy does not ignore pain, but it places pain in its proper context: temporary suffering for eternal glory. Paul's closing thoughts in this section offer us both encouragement and a challenge.

> *Live for the Day of Christ:* Let your decisions, your efforts, and your sacrifices be shaped by that final day - not by the fleeting approval of this one. Ask yourself often: Will this matter when Jesus returns?

> *View your life as an offering:* Whether you lead or follow, whether you're up front or behind the scenes, pour out your life in service to others. Let your time, talents, and treasures be spent joyfully for Christ and His church.

> *Rejoice in gospel fruit:* Celebrate what God is doing in others. Let the faithfulness of the church fill you with hope, even when your personal journey includes hardship.

> *Share in each other's joy:* We don't rejoice in isolation. Let your joy inspire others - and let their joy strengthen you. Gospel joy is communal.

Conclusion:

Paul's example in these verses is both sobering and inspiring. He shows us that the Christian life is not about avoiding sacrifice but embracing it with joy. He reminds us that when our lives are centred on Christ, even suffering becomes a platform for praise. As we wrap up this chapter, let us remember the full flow of Philippians 2:12–18:

> We are to *work out our salvation* with reverence.
> We are to *shine in the darkness* with integrity.
> We are to *pour out our lives* in joyful worship.

And through it all, we are held by the God who works in us - to will and to act for His good purpose. May we live such lives that, when Christ returns, we too may rejoice, knowing we did not run or labour in vain.

To Him be the glory, both now and forever. Amen.

7. A SERVANT'S HEART

Philippians 2:19-30 *"I hope in the Lord Jesus to send Timothy to you soon, that I also may be cheered when I receive news about you. I have no one else like him, who will show genuine concern for your welfare. For everyone looks out for their own interests, not those of Jesus Christ. But you know that Timothy has proved himself, because as a son with his father he has served with me in the work of the gospel I hope, therefore, to send him as soon as I see how things go with me. And I am confident in the Lord that I myself will come soon.*

But I think it is necessary to send back to you Epaphroditus, my brother, co-worker and fellow soldier, who is also your messenger, whom you sent to take care of my needs. For he longs for all of you and is distressed because you heard he was ill. Indeed he was ill and almost died. But God had mercy on him, and not on him only but also on me, to spare me sorrow upon sorrow. Therefore, I am all the more eager to send him, so that when you see him again you may be glad and I may have less anxiety. So then, welcome him in the Lord with great joy, and honour people like him, because he almost died for the work of Christ. He risked his life to make up for the help you yourselves could not give me."

Living Examples of the Gospel (2:19–24)

In this section, Paul introduces two of his close companions - Timothy and Epaphroditus - merely as friends or fellow workers, but as living illustrations of what he's been teaching throughout the letter.

Paul turns our attention to real people who model the humility, obedience, and sacrificial love of Christ. This reminds us that theology must be always be embodied. Sound doctrine leads to transformed lives, and Paul wants the Philippians to see it in action.

These verses overflow with affection, loyalty, and genuine discipleship. Paul begins with Timonthy and is giving the church a window into Timothy's heart - and through that, a glimpse into the kind of character we should all pursue.

1. Paul's Desire: Encouragement through Fellowship (v.19)

Paul begins by expressing his hope in the Lord to send Timothy to the Philippians soon. He longs to be "*cheered*" by the news Timothy will bring back from them. Notice the mutual encouragement here: Paul wants Timothy to bless the Philippians, and he also looks forward to being uplifted by their growth.

This reminds us that Christian leadership is never one-sided. Paul is not a distant apostle merely instructing from above. He is personally invested in the spiritual health of the church. Their joy brings him joy. Their growth renews his strength. Gospel ministry is built on deep relationship - not just messages, but mutual care.

Paul's hope is "*in the Lord Jesus,*" which is more than a pious phrase. It signals that Paul's plans are surrendered to Christ's lordship. Though Paul desires to send Timothy, he recognizes that his circumstances - and all ministry plans - are in the hands of God. This is a vital reminder for us as well: our ministry goals, our travel, our appointments, our timing - all are subject to the sovereignty of Christ. We plan, but the Lord directs our steps (Proverbs 16:9).

2. Timothy's Distinctive Character (v.20-21)

"*I have no one else like him, who will show genuine concern for your welfare.*" Here Paul makes an extraordinary statement. Among all the companions and workers around him, Timothy stands out. He is unique. Why? Because of his heart. Timothy shows *genuine concern* for others.

The Greek word which is translated here *"genuine"* (*gnēsios*) means authentic, sincere, without pretence. This is not manufactured kindness or duty-driven service. Timothy truly cares about the Philippians' welfare. He is emotionally invested in their well-being. His heart reflects the heart of Christ. Paul contrasts this with a sobering observation: *"Everyone looks out for their own interests, not those of Jesus Christ."*

This echoes Philippians 2:4, where Paul had instructed the church to look not only to their own interests but also to the interests of others. Timothy lives this out. His life is not shaped by self-advancement, but by gospel-centred service. In a world consumed with self-promotion and personal gain, this kind of person shines brightly. Timothy seeks not what is easy, but what is faithful. He puts Jesus' priorities first. That's what makes him rare - and that's what makes him valuable to Paul and to the church.

3. A Proven Servant (v.22)

"But you know that Timothy has proved himself, because as a son with his father he has served with me in the work of the gospel." Paul now points to Timothy's track record. He isn't just a promising young man with good intentions. He is tested, faithful, reliable. The Philippians had seen this firsthand when Timothy visited them during previous missionary journeys (see Acts 16–17). They *knew* his character.

Paul uses the metaphor of a father and son - not just biologically, but spiritually and ministerially. Timothy has *"served with me"* like a devoted son in his father's business. This language is deeply relational and deeply vocational. It speaks of trust, honour, mutual love, and co-labouring in the mission. The Greek word for *"served"* (*douleuō*) implies a servant's posture. Timothy was not seeking fame. He didn't consider himself above the hard work of ministry.

He served humbly, faithfully, in step with Paul, for the sake of the gospel. This is discipleship in action. Timothy didn't just listen to Paul's teaching - he followed his example, shared his burdens, and embraced the cost of ministry. And over time, he was proven faithful. He didn't burn out or bail out. He stayed the course.

4. Paul's Intentions Amid Uncertainty (v.23)

"I hope, therefore, to send him as soon as I see how things go with me." Here Paul returns to his uncertain present situation. Remember, he is in prison. His future is not yet resolved. Will he be released? Will he be executed? Will he be transferred? Rather than send Timothy immediately, Paul decides to wait until his own circumstances are clearer. But even in this uncertainty, Paul is planning, hoping, and preparing to bless the church. He isn't paralysed by his situation - he's still thinking about how to strengthen others, how to encourage their faith.

This speaks volumes about Paul's mindset. His concern is not, *"How can I be more comfortable?"* but *"How can I best serve the church?"* Whether through Timothy's presence or his own writing, Paul wants the Philippians to grow in Christ - and he's willing to delay personal comfort or clarity in order to provide that.

Timothy is more than a messenger - he is a model of Christian character. In him, we see what it looks like to live out the humility, obedience, and servant-heartedness Paul described in the earlier parts of Philippians 2.

Here are three takeaways for us:

➤ *Do we genuinely care for others' spiritual welfare?* Not just in theory, but in action - through prayer, encouragement, presence, and sacrifice?

> ➢ *Are we putting Christ's interests above our own?* Do we evaluate our choices through the lens of what will glorify Jesus and strengthen His church?

> ➢ *Are we becoming proven servants?* Faithfulness is not built overnight. It's forged through steady obedience in the same direction. Are we walking in such a way that others could point to us as trustworthy?

Timothy challenges us to move beyond surface Christianity into a life of sincere, sacrificial discipleship. His life was a living example of gospel priorities - and so should ours be.

The Apostle Paul, having just described the Christlike humility of Timothy, now lifts up another faithful servant of the gospel: Epaphroditus. While Timothy was a long-standing companion and disciple of Paul, Epaphroditus was a delegate from the Philippian church - someone Paul likely didn't know well prior to this encounter. Yet his brief time in Paul's presence left a lasting impression.

His service was so faithful and his sacrifice so complete that Paul holds him up as a model for the whole church. These few verses contain a very rich example of what gospel partnership looks like when it's marked by love, suffering, and mutual encouragement.

Epaphroditus: Brother, Co-worker, Fellow Soldier (v.25)

"But I think it is necessary to send back to you Epaphroditus - my brother, co-worker and fellow soldier, who is also your messenger, whom you sent to take care of my needs."

Paul opens this section with a string of commendations that reveal the deep value he places on Epaphroditus. These five titles are not ceremonial - they are deeply personal and theological.

> *"My brother"* – Paul calls Epaphroditus a spiritual sibling. This is more than a warm greeting. It's a recognition of their shared identity in Christ. All Christians are united in the family of God through Jesus.

> *"Co-worker"* – Epaphroditus wasn't merely a courier of gifts or letters. He rolled up his sleeves and entered into the toil of gospel ministry. He shared in the burdens of Paul's imprisonment, ministry demands, and spiritual warfare.

> *"Fellow soldier"* – This image reminds us that gospel work is not a stroll - it's a battle. Paul viewed ministry as a kind of warfare, and Epaphroditus was shoulder to shoulder with him in the trenches. There was courage and commitment in his service.

> *"Your messenger"* – Epaphroditus didn't appoint himself. He had been chosen and commissioned by the Philippian church to travel the long and dangerous road to Rome. This reminds us that churches are responsible to care for their ministers and missionaries.

> *"To take care of my needs"* – He didn't come to teach, preach, or lead - he came to serve. He willingly accepted a role of humble, personal ministry. This echoes the humility of Christ, who took on the nature of a servant (Philippians 2:7).

All these titles reveal the character of a man who embodied Philippians 2:3-4: *"Do nothing out of selfish ambition or vain conceit. Rather, in humility value others above yourselves."* Epaphroditus was a living chapter of Christlike service.

Distressed for the Church (v.26)

"For he longs for all of you and is distressed because you heard he was ill." Now Paul reveals something remarkable: even in the midst of his own suffering and serious illness, Epaphroditus was *distressed* - but not for himself.

He was distressed that the Philippians seemed worried about *him*. This gives us a glimpse into his heart. His love for the church was so deep that their anxiety over his condition caused him more anguish than his own pain.

The Greek word for *"distressed"* (*ademoneō*) is strong. It's used only a few times in the New Testament and often in reference to great emotional turmoil - the same word used of Jesus in the Garden of Gethsemane (Matthew 26:37). This isn't mild concern; it's soul-level anguish. Epaphroditus was deeply affected by the thought that the believers in Philippi were troubled by the news of his illness. His selfless concern for others reflected the mind of Christ.

It's a rare thing, even among Christians, to find someone so other-centred that they are anxious not for their health but for the emotional well-being of their church family. He longed for their comfort, their peace, and their reassurance.

He Nearly Died for the Work of Christ (v.27)

"Indeed he was ill, and almost died. But God had mercy on him, and not on him only but also on me, to spare me sorrow upon sorrow." Paul does not downplay the seriousness of Epaphroditus's condition. He confirms that *"he was ill and almost died."* The phrase implies he came to the very brink of death. We don't know what illness he contracted, but it was severe enough that his life hung in the balance.

And yet Paul, the apostle of miracles, does not focus here on divine healing. He simply says, *"God had mercy on him."* This was not automatic. It was not owed. Epaphroditus's recovery was a result of God's compassionate intervention.

What's more, Paul says it was mercy on *him* too - *"to spare me sorrow upon sorrow."* This gives us a rare glimpse into Paul's emotional vulnerability.

We sometimes think of Paul as unshakeable, almost stoic in his resolve. But here, we see a pastor with a tender heart. Losing Epaphroditus would have been an overwhelming grief for Paul, compounding the many sorrows he already endured. This reminds us that even the strongest leaders feel the weight of ministry losses. Paul doesn't hide it or spiritualize it. He admits that God's healing was a mercy that prevented crushing sorrow.

Epaphroditus may not be as well-known as Peter, John, or Timothy, but his example speaks volumes to us today.

> *Humble service is great in God's eyes.* Epaphroditus wasn't leading revivals - he was delivering aid, visiting a prisoner, helping a brother. Yet Paul heaps praise on him. No act of love done in Christ's name is small.

> *Suffering is part of gospel service.* We live in a comfort-obsessed culture, but following Jesus often means embracing risk, hardship, and loss. Epaphroditus nearly died serving Christ - and Paul sees that as honourable, not regrettable.

> *Emotional strength and gospel love go together.* Epaphroditus was both strong and tender, courageous and caring. He wept for the Philippians even while facing death. That is true gospel-shaped character.

> *Partnership matters.* Epaphroditus reminds us that the work of the gospel is not for isolated heroes - it's a team effort. Churches, messengers, and ministers all play a role.

One of the greatest ways we can apply this passage is by developing a church culture that values people like Epaphroditus - servants who may never stand on a stage but are vital to the health of the body of Christ.

Do we encourage those who serve behind the scenes? Do we honour faithful sacrifice, not just platform gifts? Do we care for our missionaries, pastors, and gospel workers when they suffer? Let's be a church that not only celebrates those who preach and lead but also those who carry burdens, travel far, and suffer quietly for the sake of Christ. In a celebrity-driven world, may we lift up and learn from the Epaphrodituses among us.

Honour the Servant-hearted (vv.28–30)

As Paul closes this section of the letter, he issues not just a practical instruction but a deep theological and pastoral appeal. He urges the Philippians to welcome Epaphroditus home - not with indifference or casual kindness, but with *great joy* and *proper honour*. In doing so, Paul reinforces a key theme from earlier in chapter 2: that true greatness in the kingdom of God is seen in self-sacrificing service.

Let's walk through these last three verses and allow Paul to reshape our understanding of what - and who - deserves celebration in the church.

Welcome him in the Lord with great joy (v28-29a)

"Therefore I am all the more eager to send him, so that when you see him again you may be glad and I may have less anxiety. So then, welcome him in the Lord with great joy…" Paul is eager to send Epaphroditus back to Philippi. This is not a disciplinary action or a retreat. It is a reunion that will bring gladness to the church and relief to Paul.

The word translated *"glad"* (*chara*) is the same root as *"joy"* (*chairo*), which runs through the entire epistle. Paul envisions this homecoming not as a sombre event, but a joyful one - filled with gratitude and celebration.

Epaphroditus is returning not defeated or broken, but victorious, having fulfilled his mission with honour. Paul wants the Philippians to *"welcome him in the Lord"* - meaning that their reception of Epaphroditus should reflect Christ's own love and appreciation. This isn't just human gratitude. It's gospel-informed joy in a faithful servant. How we receive those who have laboured for the gospel says a lot about our values as a church. Do we celebrate character or charisma? Do we rejoice in humility or only in visibility? Epaphroditus returns not with fame, but with faithfulness - and that, Paul says, is reason for great joy.

"Honour people like him" (v.29b)

"...and honour people like him..." Here, Paul moves from instruction to exhortation. He doesn't just say "welcome him" - he says "honour people like him." This isn't a one-time gesture; it's a paradigm shift. Paul is telling the church: *Make heroes out of people like Epaphroditus.* The word *"honour"* (*entimos*) conveys value, respect, and esteem. It's the same root used when describing something precious, even costly. Paul says these kinds of servants are *precious* - not only to him, but to the Lord and the church.

This directly challenges the values of both ancient and modern culture. In the Roman world, honour was reserved for the wealthy, the powerful, the accomplished. In our world, it's much the same. But Paul flips the script. In the kingdom of God, we honour those who serve, who sacrifice, who risk, who remain faithful when no one is watching.

This is a radical call to reshape our definition of greatness. We are to give public esteem and heartfelt appreciation not only to preachers and leaders, but to the selfless, often hidden workers who quietly make the gospel visible. In many churches, people like Epaphroditus are overlooked.

They may not preach, teach, or lead ministries, but they are the ones who visit the sick, clean the building, mentor the struggling, prepare meals, and give generously without being asked. Paul says: *Honour them!*

"He almost died for the work of Christ" (v.30a)

Now Paul gives the reason Epaphroditus deserves such honour. It's not about what he said or achieved - but what he was willing to suffer. He nearly died - not from carelessness or misfortune, but for the work of Christ. What a phrase! This echoes the example of Christ Himself, who became obedient to death, even death on a cross (Philippians 2:8). Paul connects Epaphroditus's sacrifice directly to Jesus' own example. His service - though not on a public stage - reflected the cruciform nature of ministry.

This is a striking reminder that every act of gospel service is a participation in the life and suffering of Christ. Whether you're preaching to thousands or delivering supplies to a missionary in prison, if it's done for Jesus, it bears eternal weight. Epaphroditus's nearness to death was not failure - it was *faithfulness*. He risked everything for the sake of Christ. He gave his health, his energy, his emotional strength - and he did it willingly. That is the kind of faithfulness that heaven applauds.

"He risked his life to make up for the help you yourselves could not give me" (v.30b)

Here Paul completes his commendation by recognizing both Epaphroditus's sacrifice and also the Philippians' intention. The church had sent him to provide help in person - support that could not be given through letters or gifts alone. In doing this, Epaphroditus literally *risked his life*. The word *"risked"* (*paraboleuomai*) is unique in the New Testament.

It carries the sense of *"exposing oneself to danger,"* even to the point of gambling one's life. Some early Christian groups - later called the *Parabolani* - actually took their name from this word. They were believers who voluntarily cared for the sick and buried the dead during times of plague, modelling their lives after Epaphroditus. In other words, Epaphroditus stared down danger and pressed forward in obedience.

This verse teaches us two important things:

> *Ministry often involves filling gaps* – Epaphroditus didn't do anything glamorous, but he did what was necessary. His mission was to stand in the gap, to carry what others couldn't carry, to serve where others couldn't go. That's real ministry.

> *Faithfulness is often risky* – Comfort, safety, and ease are not promised to gospel workers. Faithfulness may require us to leave home, endure sickness, give generously, forgive deeply, and persevere under pressure. But it is always worth it.

So how do we respond to this remarkable man?

> *Let's honour sacrificial service:* We should openly esteem and celebrate those whose lives reflect the humility and courage of Epaphroditus. In church culture, let's reserve our highest praise not for performance, but for perseverance.

> *Let's be willing to risk:* Christ is worth our comfort, our plans, and even our health if necessary. Let's not settle for safe Christianity when God is calling us to courageous faith.

➤ *Let's fill the gaps:* Look around and ask, *"Where is help needed? What burden can I carry?"* The needs of the gospel are always greater than the number of volunteers. We need more like Epaphroditus.

➤ *Let's model joyful reception and honour:* When those who serve return weary, wounded, or overlooked, let us receive them *"in the Lord with great joy,"* just as Paul commanded. Let's make the church a place where faithful servants are refreshed, not forgotten.

Conclusion

In Epaphroditus, we don't just see a man - we see a model. We see Christlike service, not shouted from a platform, but lived in the shadows. We see risk, love, humility, and endurance. And Paul says, *"Honour people like him."*

So, let's honour those around us who quietly give their all for Christ. And let's strive to be those kinds of people ourselves - whose lives echo the gospel, whose sacrifice reflects Christ, and whose faithfulness brings joy to the church and glory to God.

8. KNOWING CHRIST ABOVE ALL

Philippians 3:1-11 *"Further, my brothers and sisters, rejoice in the Lord! It is no trouble for me to write the same things to you again, and it is a safeguard for you. Watch out for those dogs, those evildoers, those mutilators of the flesh. For it is we who are the circumcision, we who serve God by his Spirit, who boast in Christ Jesus, and who put no confidence in the flesh - though I myself have reasons for such confidence. If someone else thinks they have reasons to put confidence in the flesh, I have more: circumcised on the eighth day, of the people of Israel, of the tribe of Benjamin, a Hebrew of Hebrews; in regard to the law, a Pharisee; as for zeal, persecuting the church; as for righteousness based on the law, faultless.*

But whatever were gains to me I now consider loss for the sake of Christ. What is more, I consider everything a loss because of the surpassing worth of knowing Christ Jesus my Lord, for whose sake I have lost all things. I consider them garbage, that I may gain Christ and be found in him, not having a righteousness of my own that comes from the law, but that which is through faith in Christ - the righteousness that comes from God on the basis of faith.

I want to know Christ - yes, to know the power of his resurrection and participation in his sufferings, becoming like him in his death, and so, somehow, attaining to the resurrection from the dead."

Introduction: Joy and Discernment

Paul opens Philippians 3 with a return to one of his major themes - joy. But this joy is not a fleeting emotion. It's the stance of the soul rooted in Christ, and it's not divorced from discernment. In fact, in the next breath, Paul moves from *"rejoice in the Lord"* to a strong warning about spiritual deception.

This pairing may seem strange at first - joy and warning. But in the Christian life, they go hand in hand. True joy isn't naïve; it's *guarded*. Paul knew that rejoicing in Christ required clarity about who Christ is and what He has done - and that clarity was under threat in Philippi.

Rejoice in the Lord – Not in Ourselves (v.1)

"Further, my brothers and sisters, rejoice in the Lord! It is no trouble for me to write the same things to you again, and it is a safeguard for you." Paul opens with this very clear imperative: *"Rejoice in the Lord!"* This is not a suggestion. It is a command to centre our joy in *who Christ is* and *what He has done.* Christian joy is never anchored in circumstances - it's always anchored in the Lord. And because Christ doesn't change, our joy doesn't have to.

Then Paul adds something curious: *"It is no trouble for me to write the same things to you again, and it is a safeguard for you."* Apparently, Paul had previously taught or written about the things he's about to say, and he doesn't mind repeating them. Why? Because they serve as a *safeguard* - a spiritual protection against false teaching and misplaced confidence.

There's a lesson here for every believer and every church: we need repetition. We need reminders. Because we forget, we drift. Because the world, the flesh, and the devil are constantly tempting us to place our confidence somewhere other than in Christ.

Watch Out – Strong Warnings Against Legalism (v.2)

"Watch out for those dogs, those evildoers, those mutilators of the flesh." This is one of Paul's sharpest warnings in the entire letter. He doesn't name names, but the language is intense. He gives three rapid-fire warnings - each more pointed than the last.

- ➢ *"Watch out for those dogs"* - In Jewish culture, dogs were unclean scavengers - not the friendly household pets we think of today. Paul uses this term to describe the very people who would have called *Gentile* Christians "dogs" - those who insisted that Gentiles must adopt Jewish practices, particularly circumcision, in order to be fully accepted by God. Paul turns the insult around. He's saying, *No, they're the unclean ones.*

- ➢ *"Watch out for those evildoers"* – These people claimed to be teaching righteousness, but Paul says they're actually promoting evil. Why? Because they were undermining the sufficiency of Christ by adding human effort to salvation.

- ➢ *"Watch out for those mutilators of the flesh"* – This is a direct attack on those who insisted that circumcision was required for salvation. Paul plays on the Greek word for circumcision (*peritomē*) and changes it to *katatomē*, which means mutilation. He's saying, *"What they're doing isn't a sacred sign - it's pointless, harmful cutting."*

What's the danger here? Legalism. Now legalism is not just strict living - it's the belief that your right standing with God is based on your performance. It may use Christian language. It may appeal to religious tradition. But Paul sees it as a deadly threat to the gospel.

True Identity in Christ (v.3)

"For it is we who are the circumcision, we who serve God by his Spirit, who boast in Christ Jesus, and who put no confidence in the flesh." Here, Paul flips the script entirely. The false teachers claimed to be the true *"circumcision"* - the true people of God.

But Paul declares that the real people of God are those who are circumcised in heart, not just in flesh (see Romans 2:29). And he defines them in three ways:

> ➢ *"We who serve God by his Spirit"* - True worship isn't confined to ritual or location. It flows from the Holy Spirit dwelling in the believer, transforming worship from duty to delight.

> ➢ *"Who boast in Christ Jesus"* - True believers don't boast in their own righteousness, status, or religious record. They boast in Christ alone. Paul will expand on this theme in the following verses as he lists his own impressive résumé.

> ➢ *"Who put no confidence in the flesh"* - This is the heart of Paul's argument. The flesh - our human ability, lineage, effort, or credentials - is not a safe place to trust. It might look impressive, but it cannot save. Only Christ can.

This verse is a clear summary of Paul's gospel: Salvation is by grace through faith, not by works. And the evidence of that salvation is Spirit-empowered worship, Christ-centred boasting, and a deep rejection of self-reliance.

In these first three verses of Philippians 3, Paul gives us a powerful reminder: real joy and spiritual discernment go hand in hand. To rejoice in the Lord is not to ignore danger but to root ourselves so deeply in Christ that we recognize and reject all false substitutes. We live in a world that constantly tempts us to measure ourselves by performance, popularity, or religious activity.

But the gospel says: *Your confidence must be in Christ alone.* No amount of rule-keeping, ritual, or résumé can give you peace with God. Only Jesus can. So let us rejoice in Him. Let us watch out for false confidences.

And let us be people who worship by the Spirit, boast in Christ, and put no confidence in the flesh.

What Was to My Gain, I Now Count as Loss (vv. 4–8a)

In the opening verses of Philippians 3, Paul passionately warned the church against placing confidence in human effort, status, or religious performance. He reminded them that true believers are those who serve God by His Spirit, boast in Christ, and put no confidence in the flesh.

Now, in verses 4-8a, Paul shifts gears. He moves from warning to personal testimony. If anyone had reason to place confidence in the flesh, it was Paul. His résumé, by every Jewish standard, was flawless.

But now he looks at that same résumé - and he calls it loss. This section is one of the most profound personal statements in all of Paul's letters. It is both autobiographical and theological. Paul wants us to see, with unmistakable clarity, that knowing Christ is infinitely better than anything else we could ever achieve, possess, or boast in.

Paul's Former Confidence in the Flesh (v.4–6)

Paul begins with a bold statement: *"If anyone had the right to put confidence in human credentials, I did."* And he proceeds to list seven qualifications - four of them inherited and three achieved - that once formed the foundation of his self-righteousness.

a. Four inherited advantages:

➤ *"Circumcised on the eighth day"* – Paul was born into the covenant, not converted into it later. He fulfilled the Jewish law from infancy.

➤ *"Of the people of Israel"* – He wasn't a Gentile convert or a proselyte; he was born into God's chosen people.

- ➤ *"Of the tribe of Benjamin"* – A prestigious tribe that gave Israel its first king (Saul) and remained loyal to the house of David. Paul's lineage was honourable and notable.

- ➤ *"A Hebrew of Hebrews"* – Paul was raised in strict observance of Hebrew culture, language, and religion. He was not influenced by Hellenism or compromise.

b. Three personal achievements:

- ➤ *"In regard to the law, a Pharisee"* – Paul belonged to the most rigorous sect of Judaism. He was deeply committed to the law, both written and oral.

- ➤ *"As for zeal, persecuting the church"* – Paul wasn't just intellectually committed - he was passionately active. His zeal led him to hunt down Christians, thinking he was defending God's truth.

- ➤ *"As for righteousness based on the law, faultless"* – By external standards, Paul kept the law impeccably. He was blameless in his observance of rules and rituals.

Taken together, this list is impressive. In his former life, Paul would have been admired, respected, and envied. He had pedigree, passion, and performance. But something happened - something that radically altered how he viewed all of it.

A Dramatic Reversal: From Gain to Loss (v.7)

"But whatever were gains to me I now consider loss for the sake of Christ." This is one of the most important turning points in Paul's life - and in this letter. The word *"gains"* is in the plural - Paul saw all his credentials as accumulating spiritual credit. But now, in Christ, Paul must re-evaluate everything. *"I now consider [them] loss."*

This is the language of accounting. Paul is talking about spiritual bookkeeping. What once was in the *'asset'* column of his life - line after line of religious achievement, has now been moved to the *'liability'* column. It's not just that those things are neutral, even harmful if they keep you from relying on Christ.

This is radical. Paul isn't comparing sin with Christ - he's comparing his best religious works with Christ and still finds them worthless by comparison. Why? Because none of those things could give him righteousness. None of them could cleanse his sin. None of them could reconcile him to God. Only Jesus could

Paul's testimony forces us to ask: *What's in my 'gain' column?* What am I tempted to boast in, depend on, or take pride in? Our culture may not boast in religious heritage like Paul's, but we have our own lists - moralism, success, church attendance, ministry titles, charitable giving, theological knowledge. But if any of those become a substitute for Christ - or a source of spiritual pride - they must be counted as loss.

The Surpassing Worth of Christ (v.8a)

"What is more, I consider everything a loss because of the surpassing worth of knowing Christ Jesus my Lord..." Paul doesn't stop at the previous list. He now expands the scope. Not just his Jewish heritage or religious efforts - but everything is counted as loss. Every accomplishment, every credential, every achievement - no matter how impressive - is worthless compared to Christ. Why? Because of the *surpassing worth* of knowing Christ Jesus my Lord.

Notice the deeply personal language here. Paul doesn't say, *"knowing about Christ"* or *"believing the doctrines of Christ."* He says *knowing Christ Jesus my Lord.*

This is not mere theology - it is relationship. Christ is not just an idea or a figure in history. He is my Lord - my Saviour, my Master, my Treasure. The Greek word here for *"knowing"* (*gnōsis*) actually conveys intimate, experiential knowledge. It's not just head knowledge; it's relational knowledge.

Paul is describing a deep, abiding, joyful union with Jesus that overshadows all else. This is the heart of Christianity - not rule-keeping, not tradition, not credentials, but it is knowing Christ. That is the treasure. That is the goal. That is the surpassing worth.

In these verses, Paul is offering more than a personal testimony - he is offering a new value system. He invites us to view our lives through the lens of the gospel and to ask: *What truly matters? What do I count as gain? What am I clinging to?* When we see Christ clearly - His beauty, grace, power, love, and righteousness - everything else fades into the background. Not because those things are inherently bad, but because Christ is infinitely better. So let us follow Paul's example. Let us gladly lay down every lesser confidence. Let us stop boasting in ourselves. And let us rejoice in the all-surpassing worth of knowing Christ Jesus our Lord.

Sharing in His Sufferings, Becoming Like Him (vv. 8b–11)

Up to this point in Philippians 3, Paul has dismantled every basis for human confidence and exalted the supreme value of knowing Christ. But now, he presses deeper. Paul doesn't only desire knowledge *about* Christ or even to belong *to* Christ - he longs to *experience* Christ in His fullness.

This final portion of our passage is perhaps the most personal and passionate section of Paul's writing.

He invites us to embrace a faith that is not content with status or security, but one that enters directly into Christ's suffering, His death, and ultimately, His resurrection. This is not a casual association. This is radical identification with Jesus - one that reshapes every aspect of our life.

"I have lost all things" (v.8b)

"For whose sake I have lost all things. I consider them garbage, that I may gain Christ..." Earlier in verse 7, Paul said he considered his former gains as loss. Now in verse 8, he takes it even further: *I have lost all things.* This is not theory - it is Paul's lived reality. Since coming to Christ, Paul had lost his reputation, his status as a respected Pharisee, his community, and his freedom.

He was writing this very letter from prison. He had suffered beatings, shipwrecks, hunger, betrayal, and near-death experiences - all for the sake of the gospel.

And yet, what does he call those losses? *Garbage.* The Greek word here (*skubalon*) is unusually strong. It can mean rubbish, refuse, or even excrement. It's what you step in accidently in the cow paddock! That's what Paul thinks of his greatest achievements! It's intentionally shocking. Paul isn't being polite - he's showing how utterly worthless his old life is compared to the treasure he now possesses in Christ.

Why such strong language? Because Paul has found something *infinitely better.* He says, "that I may gain Christ..." In other words, everything else is rubbish if it stands in the way of gaining more of Jesus. What a profound challenge for us. We live in a culture that prizes success, wealth, comfort, and recognition. But Paul says: *Even if you had it all, it would be garbage compared to gaining Christ.* That's the mark of a heart that treasures Jesus above all else.

Being found in Him (v.9)

"...and be found in him, not having a righteousness of my own that comes from the law, but that which is through faith in Christ - the righteousness that comes from God on the basis of faith." This is the theological heart of the gospel. Paul contrasts two kinds of righteousness:

➢ *"My own righteousness" that comes from the law* - This is the kind of righteousness that is earned, performed, and maintained through obedience. It's external, fragile, and ultimately insufficient.

➢ *"The righteousness that comes from God on the basis of faith"* - This is the righteousness that God gives as a gift to those who trust in Jesus. It's not earned - it's *imputed*. Christ's righteousness is credited to us by faith.

This doctrine is the cornerstone of salvation: *Justification by grace through faith.* Paul doesn't just affirm it doctrinally - he *cherishes* it. He says his greatest joy is to be found in Christ, clothed not in his own achievements but in the righteousness of Jesus. This is what allows us to stand before a holy God - not our spiritual résumé, but Christ's perfect record applied to us.

That's why Paul says he has no confidence in the flesh - because it could never give him what he truly needed: righteousness from God. And that righteousness is received not by trying harder, but by trusting completely in Christ.

"I want to know Christ" (v.10a)

"I want to know Christ - yes, to know the power of his resurrection..." Here we come to the emotional climax of Paul's testimony: *"I want to know Christ."* Remember, Paul is not a new believer. He has walked with Jesus for decades.

He has planted churches, written Scripture, and endured much for the gospel. Yet his heart still cries out, *"I want to know Him."*

This is the lifelong pursuit of the believer - not just knowledge about Christ, but personal, experiential, relational knowing. Paul yearns to go deeper into the mystery, majesty, and intimacy of union with Jesus.

Specifically, Paul says he wants to know *"the power of his resurrection."* This power is not just a future hope, but a present reality. It is the same power that raised Jesus from the dead, and it now lives in us through the Holy Spirit (see Romans 8:11). This resurrection power:

- Brings dead hearts to life
- Breaks the power of sin
- Sustains us in suffering
- Enables obedience
- Fills us with hope
- Guarantees future glory

To know Christ is to live in this resurrection power every day - not by human strength, but by divine enablement.

"And participation in his sufferings" (v.10b)

"...and participation in his sufferings, becoming like him in his death..." This is the part of knowing Christ that many would prefer to skip. Yet Paul embraces it. He desires not just resurrection power, but *participation in Christ's sufferings.* The Greek word here for *"participation"* is *koinonia* - the same word used for fellowship. Paul wants to share in Christ's sufferings, not out of masochism, but because it brings him closer to the heart of the Saviour.

To suffer for Christ is to walk the path that He walked - to lay down our rights, endure rejection, serve others, and remain faithful in trials. In doing so, we are *being conformed to His death* - dying to self, pride, and worldly ambition.

Suffering is not an interruption to the Christian life - it's part of the pattern. And through it, we come to know Christ more deeply, because we experience something of what He experienced.

"And so, somehow, attaining to the resurrection" (v.11)

"...and so, somehow, attaining to the resurrection from the dead." Paul ends this section with a humble, hopeful statement. He says that through knowing Christ - both in power and in suffering – Paul is looking forward to sharing in Christ's resurrection.

The word *"somehow"* doesn't indicate doubt about the resurrection itself. Rather, it expresses Paul's awe and humility about the process. He's not presuming upon his future; he is pressing into it with hope and longing.

This is Paul's ultimate goal - to rise with Christ, to be glorified, to be made fully like Him in every way. It's not just about escape from death - it's about union with Jesus forever.

Conclusion:

In this final section of Philippians 3:1–11, Paul paints a stunning portrait of Christian faith - not as mere belief, but as total identification with Christ.

➢ He counts all things as loss for the sake of knowing Jesus.

➢ He wants to be found in Christ, clothed in His righteousness.

➤ He desires to know Christ's power and participate in His suffering.

➤ He looks forward to resurrection with Jesus in glory.

This is not comfortable Christianity. This is not half-hearted discipleship. This is a life utterly consumed with Christ - a life that sees Jesus as the surpassing treasure above all.

So let us ask ourselves:

➤ Do we treasure Christ like this?

➤ Are we willing to lose what the world values to gain what only Christ can give?

➤ Are we seeking to know Him - not just in theology, but in the trenches of suffering and obedience?

May the Spirit stir in us the same longing that filled Paul's heart. And may we, like him, count everything as loss compared to the surpassing worth of knowing Christ Jesus our Lord.

9. PRESSING ON TOWARD THE GOAL

Philippians 3:12-16 *"Not that I have already obtained all this, or have already arrived at my goal, but I press on to take hold of that for which Christ Jesus took hold of me. Brothers and sisters, I do not consider myself yet to have taken hold of it. But one thing I do: Forgetting what is behind and straining toward what is ahead, I press on toward the goal to win the prize for which God has called me heavenward in Christ Jesus. All of us, then, who are mature should take such a view of things. And if on some point you think differently, that too God will make clear to you. Only let us live up to what we have already attained."*

Not Yet Perfect, But Always Pressing On (v.12)

By the time we reach this section of Philippians 3, Paul has laid out a remarkable testimony. He's shown us the surpassing value of knowing Christ, the futility of trusting in the flesh, and the transforming power of Christ's resurrection. But lest anyone think he considers himself already *"arrived"* or fully sanctified, Paul immediately clarifies his spiritual posture: *"Not that I have already obtained all this..."*

The Apostle Paul - church planter, theologian, martyr, author of the majority of the New Testament - wants the Philippians (and us) to know that he is still on the journey. The great Apostle is not resting on past accomplishments. He is not paralysed by past failures. Instead, he is pressing on, straining forward, and pursuing the ultimate prize: full communion with Christ. This is a message we desperately need in our time. In a culture of spiritual complacency, instant gratification, and shallow Christianity, Paul calls us to a different mindset - a mindset of progress, growth, humility, and holy ambition.

"Not that I have already obtained all this..." (v.12a)

"Not that I have already obtained all this or have already arrived at my goal..." Paul begins with an honest admission. Despite his maturity, his obedience, and his passion for Christ, he confesses: *"I have not arrived."* This statement is striking, not just because of who Paul is, but because of how rare this attitude is in our day. Many Christians grow content with a baseline level of spirituality. They attend church, avoid scandalous sins, and consider themselves settled. But Paul refuses to settle. He lives with a holy discontent - not driven by guilt or legalism, but by the sheer greatness of Christ and the glory of what lies ahead.

The phrase *"already obtained"* most likely refers back to the fullness of resurrection life and perfect conformity to Christ that he discussed in verses 10-11. Paul knows he has not yet reached the end. He has not been fully made like Christ. He has not yet experienced the resurrection. Therefore, he presses on.

There is something deeply humbling and inspiring about this confession. Paul is modelling a key truth: Spiritual maturity is not about perfection - it's about pursuit. The mark of a mature believer is not that they think they've arrived, but that they press forward with urgency and humility.

"But I press on to take hold of that for which Christ Jesus took hold of me." (v.12b)

This is the heartbeat of Paul's spiritual life: *"I press on."* The Greek word here (*diōkō*) conveys intense pursuit, like a runner chasing a goal or a hunter tracking prey. It's not casual - it's focused and determined. Paul is not coasting through the Christian life. He's not treating faith as a side interest. He is pursuing Christ with every fibre of his being. And why? Because Christ Jesus took hold of him.

This is one of the most beautiful phrases in this passage: *"To take hold of that for which Christ Jesus took hold of me."* Paul is not striving to earn Christ's love - he already has it. He's not chasing salvation - he's already been seized by grace. But now, having been gripped by Christ, Paul really wants to grasp everything Christ has for him.

There's a powerful tension here: Paul acknowledges that Christ acted first - He *"took hold"* of Paul on the Damascus Road, transforming him from persecutor to preacher, from self-righteous Pharisee to Christ-exalting apostle. But that initial moment of grace now fuels Paul's lifelong pursuit of the One who saved him. This is the shape of every true Christian life:

> Christ takes hold of us by grace.

> Then we spend the rest of our lives pressing in, pressing forward, pressing on - to lay hold of Him more fully, to become more like Him, and to finish the race He has set before us.

3. Saved by Grace, Pressing on in Grace

This verse also helps us to understand a really crucial balance in Christian theology: the relationship between God's initiative and our response.

> Salvation is entirely by grace. Christ *"took hold"* of us first. We did not earn it, initiate it, or deserve it.

> But that grace produces a response. We now live to take hold of the very purpose for which He saved us. (see 1 Corinthians 15:10)

Paul isn't contradicting his earlier statements about justification by faith. He's not saying we must now earn what we've been given.

Rather, he's showing us that grace is not opposed to effort - it's opposed to earning. To "press on" is not to panic or perform, but to pursue Christ out of love, gratitude, and awe. This is what separates gospel-driven perseverance from works-based religion. The former is joyful, Spirit-empowered, and full of hope. The latter is anxious, self-reliant, and never enough. Paul's example urges us to avoid two great errors in the Christian life:

> *Complacency:* thinking we've arrived, when in truth we've just begun.

> *Despair:* believing we'll never change, when in truth Christ is at work in us.

Instead, we press on - with confidence that Christ has taken hold of us, and with determination to grow more fully into His likeness.

This first verse of our passage (Philippians 3:12) is packed with gospel clarity and spiritual passion. It shows us that the Christian life is a race still being run, not a prize already possessed. Paul's humility *("Not that I have already obtained...")* reminds us that no one is above the need for growth. His urgency *("I press on...")* challenges us to refuse spiritual stagnation. And his gospel foundation *("...because Christ Jesus took hold of me")* anchors all our striving in the finished work of Jesus.

So, what does this mean for us today?

> If you feel stuck in your faith, take heart: You are not alone. Even Paul said he hadn't arrived. But don't stay stuck. Press on.

> If you've been relying on past spiritual victories, remember that yesterday's faithfulness is not enough for today's journey. Press on.

➤ If you are overwhelmed by how far you have to go, remember: Christ has taken hold of you. And He will complete what He started. So, press on.

Let this be your prayer today: *"Lord Jesus, since You have taken hold of me, help me to take hold of everything You desire for me. I'm not there yet - but I will press on, until I see You face to face."*

Forgetting What Is Behind and Straining Toward What Is Ahead (vv. 13–14)

Paul has just declared in verse 12 that he hasn't already obtained his ultimate goal. He acknowledges that he is still in process - still being shaped into the likeness of Christ. Now, in verses 13 and 14, Paul expands that thought by using a powerful metaphor drawn from the world of athletics. He pictures the Christian life as a race. The runner has one aim: to reach the finish line and win the prize.

The picture is full of energy, direction, and determination. There's no drifting here, no passive waiting. Paul models for us a faith that moves forward intentionally. He invites us to adopt a mindset that refuses to dwell in the past and instead embraces a relentless pursuit of Christ.

A Humble Acknowledgment: (v.13a)

Paul begins verse 13 by repeating and reinforcing what he said in verse 12: *"I do not consider myself yet to have taken hold of it."* The repetition is deliberate. Paul wants the Philippians to be absolutely clear: he is still growing. This is an incredible statement coming from the Apostle Paul. If *he* hasn't arrived - if *he* still sees room to grow - then surely none of us should consider ourselves spiritually finished. It's a powerful reminder that spiritual maturity includes a deep awareness of how far we still have to go.

There's no arrogance here. No spiritual entitlement. Just the humble confession of a man who is deeply in love with Jesus and who knows he still has more of Christ to experience. That humility is not defeatist - it's what fuels Paul's pursuit. Because he knows he hasn't yet arrived, he keeps striving toward what lies ahead.

The Power of Focus: "But one thing I do..." (v.13b)

This next phrase is crucial: *"But one thing I do..."* In Greek, the structure is even more emphatic - Paul is saying, *"But one thing!"* This is all about singular focus, undivided attention, total commitment. Paul is not distracted by lesser pursuits. His life is not pulled in ten different directions. His heart is locked on one goal: to know Christ more fully and to become like Him. All other ambitions have been subordinated to this one aim.

This reminds us of Psalm 27:4, where David says, *"One thing I ask from the Lord, this only do I seek..."* It echoes the words of Jesus to Martha in Luke 10:42, *"Only one thing is necessary."* The most faithful saints in Scripture were those who lived with focused devotion.

We are constantly tempted to live divided lives - trying to serve God while also pursuing comfort, recognition, or personal achievement. But Paul says, *"One thing."* That's what defines the life of faith. A singular passion for Christ and His calling.

Letting Go: "Forgetting what is behind..." (v.13c)

Here is one of the most challenging and liberating principles in the Christian life: *"forgetting what is behind."* Paul doesn't mean literal amnesia. He's not suggesting that we erase our memory. He means that we must refuse to let the past define or control us.

The past - whether good or bad - can become a burden that holds us back from running freely. For Paul, this meant letting go of:

➢ *His past achievements* - his status as a Pharisee, his reputation, his zeal. All of that, once a source of pride, now counted as loss.

➢ *His past failures* - his persecution of the church, his complicity in Stephen's death, his misplaced zeal. These could have crippled him with shame, but he laid them down at the foot of the cross.

We, too, must forget what is behind:

➢ Let go of *past sins*, trusting that Christ's blood is enough to cleanse you.

➢ Let go of *past glories*, refusing to rest on yesterday's victories.

➢ Let go of *past wounds*, surrendering bitterness and trusting God's healing.

Only when we release the past can we be free to run the race set before us.

"Straining toward what is ahead..." (v.13d)

The verb *"straining"* here evokes the image of a runner stretching out toward the finish line, every muscle taut, every nerve engaged. This is not a casual jog - it is an intense effort, full of passion and urgency. Christian growth is not automatic. It requires spiritual effort, not to earn salvation, but in response to it. We strive toward greater intimacy with Christ, deeper obedience, stronger faith, and more faithful service. What's ahead? More of Christ. More of His likeness. More opportunities to serve. More of His kingdom breaking into the world.

Paul is not content with a static faith. He wants to keep growing until the day he sees Jesus face to face. This image invites us to examine our lives. Are we reaching forward, or are we standing still? Are we spiritually coasting, or are we pressing in?

The Finish Line: "I press on toward the goal to win the prize..." (v.14a)

Now Paul returns to the theme of verse 12: *"I press on."* The Christian life is not a sprint - it's a long-distance race. And the goal is clear: *"to win the prize for which God has called me heavenward in Christ Jesus."* What is the prize? It is full and final union with Christ. It is hearing, *"Well done, good and faithful servant."* It is receiving the crown of righteousness that the Lord has promised to those who love Him (2 Timothy 4:8). It is the upward call of God - the invitation to glory, the summons to eternity.

This *"heavenward call"* gives shape and motivation to everything we do on earth. Paul lived every day in light of that future. And so should we. The prize is not worldly success, not human applause, not even moral achievement. The prize is Christ Himself. In these two verses, Paul gives us a vivid picture of the Christian life:

➢ It's a life of *humility* - recognizing we haven't arrived.

➢ A life of *focus* - pursuing one thing above all else.

➢ A life of *release* - letting go of what's behind.

➢ A life of *effort* - straining forward.

➢ A life of *hope* - pressing toward the prize.

So, how do we live this way? By keeping our eyes on Jesus. He is both the finish line and the running partner. He is the One who called us and the One who will bring us safely home.

Let us, like Paul, press on - joyfully, passionately, and persistently - toward the upward call of God in Christ Jesus.

Maturity and Unity in the Race (vv. 15-16)

Paul has just described the Christian life as a race - a focused pursuit of Christ in which we forget the past and strain toward what lies ahead. But now, in verses 15 and 16, he shifts from personal testimony to corporate encouragement. He turns to the Philippians and says, in effect, *"Let's run this race together."*

These verses offer us a clear vision for Christian maturity and a call to unity in the journey of faith. Paul shows us that pressing on toward the goal isn't just an individual pursuit - it's a community effort. We are called to grow in Christ together, to encourage one another, and to walk in the truth we already know. Let's explore three key exhortations from these verses.

➢ The Call to Maturity (v.15a)

"All of us, then, who are mature should take such a view of things." Paul uses the word "then" (or "therefore") to connect verse 15 to what he has just said. In other words, *"In light of everything I've just described - the humble pursuit of Christ, the letting go of the past, the straining toward what is ahead - this is how mature believers should think."*

The Greek word for *"mature"* here (*teleioi*) can also be translated as *"perfect,"* but clearly Paul doesn't mean sinless perfection. After all, in verse 12, he just said, *"Not that I have already been made perfect."* What Paul means here is spiritual maturity - a mindset shaped by the gospel, grounded in humility, and hungry for growth. This is an important reminder that maturity is not marked by how much you know, but by how you think.

A mature Christian doesn't believe they've arrived. A mature Christian doesn't become complacent. Instead, they adopt the same mindset Paul describes:

➢ *I haven't arrived.*

➢ *I'm still growing.*

➢ *I want more of Christ.*

➢ *I'm pressing on toward the goal.*

Paul is urging the Philippians - and us - to cultivate this kind of thinking. Not a mindset of defeat or apathy, but one of passionate pursuit and eager expectation. This is the mark of a gospel-shaped life.

➢ The Grace for Growth (v.15b)

"And if on some point you think differently, that too God will make clear to you." This is a beautiful example of Paul's pastoral wisdom and leadership. He acknowledges that not everyone in the church may yet see things the same way. Some may still be clinging to their religious credentials. Others may be spiritually immature or uncertain. 1But instead of rebuking them harshly or demanding instant agreement, Paul expresses confidence in God's work in them: *"That too God will make clear to you."*

What a powerful lesson in humility and patience. Paul knows that spiritual growth is a process, and that it is ultimately God who always brings understanding and transformation. This frees us from the pressure to argue people into maturity. Yes, we should teach truth clearly and correct gently when necessary. But we must also trust the Holy Spirit to do the deeper work of conviction and growth. Paul's tone here is not defensive or argumentative - it's calm, trusting, and confident in God's timing. That's how mature believers speak.

That's how gospel-centred communities grow - through truth spoken in love, and through space for the Spirit to work. If you find yourself frustrated that others don't "get it" the way you do, remember this verse. If you're wrestling with questions yourself, take comfort - God will make it clear in His time, as you remain open to His leading.

➤ Living What We Already Know (v.16)

This verse is both encouraging and challenging. Paul is saying, *"Wherever you are in your walk with Christ - however much you already understand - make sure you're living it."* In other words, don't wait until you know everything to start obeying what you already know. Spiritual maturity is not just about revelation - it's about application.

Many Christians are hungry for more knowledge, but Paul is urging us to walk faithfully in what we've already been taught. This guards against two dangers:

➤ *Pride*: thinking that knowing more makes us mature, even if we're not living it out.

➤ *Stagnation*: waiting for deeper insight before we start obeying clear commands.

God calls us to put our faith into action. If we know we are to forgive, we must forgive. If we know we are to serve, we must serve. If we know we are to press on, we must not settle. This is also an invitation to consistency.

Paul is calling the Philippians to remain faithful to the gospel they have already received and the progress they've already made. He wants them to keep growing - but not to forget or neglect what they already understand. In short, Paul is saying: *Keep walking in the light you've been given, and God will provide more.*

Conclusion:

Philippians 3:15-16 closes this powerful passage on spiritual pursuit with a call to maturity, unity, and consistency. It shows us that:

> ➢ *Mature believers keep pressing on* - they don't pretend to have arrived.

> ➢ *Mature believers give grace to others* - they trust God to guide those who differ.

> ➢ *Mature believers walk in obedience* - they live out what they already know.

In a culture that often prizes appearance over authenticity, and knowledge over obedience, Paul offers a refreshing and radical alternative. He paints a picture of a church that is humble, focused, gracious, and growing - not alone, but together.

Let this be our prayer:

Lord, give us the mind of maturity. Help us to press on, to think rightly, to love patiently, and to walk faithfully. Keep us united in pursuit of the upward call of God in Christ Jesus. Amen.

10. CITIZENS OF HEAVEN

Philippians 3:17-21 *"Join together in following my example, brothers and sisters, and just as you have us as a model, keep your eyes on those who live as we do. For, as I have often told you before and now tell you again even with tears, many live as enemies of the cross of Christ. Their destiny is destruction, their god is their stomach, and their glory is in their shame. Their mind is set on earthly things. But our citizenship is in heaven. And we eagerly await a Savior from there, the Lord Jesus Christ, who, by the power that enables him to bring everything under his control, will transform our lowly bodies so that they will be like his glorious body."*

Introduction: The Imitation We All Need

We live in a world filled with influencers. Every day, we are each being shaped - consciously and unconsciously - by the people we follow. Whether it's celebrities, politicians, pastors, or peers, the examples we watch inevitably shape our desires, choices, and identities. Imitation is hard-wired into human nature. Paul understood this truth long before social media ever existed. He knew that spiritual growth doesn't happen in a vacuum.

It happens through relationships. It also happens through example. Through watching and following others who are following Christ. That's why Paul says in Philippians 3:17: *"Join together in following my example, brothers and sisters, and just as you have us as a model, keep your eyes on those who live as we do."*

This isn't pride or arrogance - it's spiritual leadership. Paul is saying, *"If you want to grow in Christ, look at how I live - and find others who are walking the same path."*

In doing so, he gives us a powerful truth: God uses people to shape people. Let's unpack three truths from this verse about godly imitation.

"Join together" – A Community Pursuit

Paul begins with the phrase, *"Join together…"* This is not a private command. It's a collective invitation. The Christian journey was never meant to be walked alone. From start to finish, the Bible presents faith as a shared journey. The Greek word used here (*symmimetai*) is translated as *"join in imitating."* It's plural - addressed to the whole church. Paul is inviting the Philippians to corporately imitate godly examples, not in isolation, but in community. Why is this so important? Because spiritual growth is not just about information - it's about transformation through imitation. And imitation happens best in relationships.

You learn to pray by praying with others. You learn to serve by watching people serve. You learn to forgive, to love, to persevere - by walking alongside people who model those things. Too many Christians try to grow in isolation. They read books, attend services, and consume teaching - but they're not *walking with* other believers. Paul says: *Don't go it alone. Join together. Follow the example of mature believers in your community.* This is why small groups, discipleship relationships, and mentoring are so vital in the church. You don't grow by merely hearing about Christ - you grow by watching Him reflected in the lives of His people.

"In following my example"

Some people might feel uncomfortable with Paul's statement: *"Follow my example."* Isn't that a bit self-promoting? Not at all. In fact, it's deeply biblical. Paul isn't saying, *"I'm perfect."* Just a few verses earlier (v.12), he admitted he hadn't yet "taken hold" of everything.

But he's saying, *"I'm pursuing Christ. Follow my direction, follow my pattern, and you'll grow too."* Elsewhere, Paul makes the same appeal:

> ➤ *"Follow my example, as I follow the example of Christ."* (1 Corinthians 11:1)

> ➤ *"Whatever you have learned or received or heard from me or seen in me - put it into practice."* (Philippians 4:9)

> ➤ *"You became imitators of us and of the Lord…"* (1 Thessalonians 1:6)

This is the biblical model of discipleship. We learn Christ by imitating those who are imitating Christ. We're not called to perfection, but to progress - and godly leaders help point the way. This raises a question for each of us:

Who are you following? Are there mature believers in your life whose example you're watching and learning from? Do you have mentors, spiritual fathers or mothers, people who challenge and encourage you? If not, it's time to seek them out. Ask God to bring into your life those whose walk can strengthen your own. It also raises another question:

Who is following you? Whether you realise it or not, someone is watching your example. What are they learning from you about humility, prayer, integrity, and love? As we grow in maturity, we should not only follow examples - we should become them. Paul wasn't special - he was simply available, intentional, and Christ-centred. You can be the same.

"Keep your eyes on those who live as we do"

Paul expands the command beyond himself: *"Keep your eyes on those who live as we do."* He's saying, *"I'm not the only one. There are others living faithfully. Watch them. Learn from them. Let their example shape you."* This is incredibly important. We need multiple models of faith.

No single person reflects the fullness of Christ, but together, we form a fuller picture. In every healthy church, there should be people - men and women, young and old - who are living lives worthy of imitation.

People who don't just know the truth but embody it. People who are growing, not perfect; who radiate joy, compassion, and conviction. Paul says, *"Keep your eyes on them."* Be watchful. Be intentional. Let yourself be discipled by watching their example.

This also implies that we must be discerning about who we follow. The world is full of loud voices, but not all are trustworthy. Just because someone has a platform doesn't mean they have character. Just because someone teaches well doesn't mean they live well.

Paul says: *"Watch the people whose lives match the gospel. Follow the ones who live like we do - who model Christ."*

Philippians 3:17 gives us a vision for spiritual growth that is deeply relational and rooted in community. It reminds us that:

➤ We grow best *together*, not alone.

➤ God gives us *examples* to follow, so we can learn how to live the faith.

➤ We are called to *watch carefully*, imitate wisely, and become examples ourselves.

So let me ask you:

➤ Who are you watching?

➤ Who are you walking with?

➤ Who are you becoming?

God calls us to follow Him by following others who are faithfully walking in His steps. Let us join together in imitating those who walk with Christ - and let us strive to become the kind of people whose lives are worth imitating.

Enemies of the Cross – A Sorrowful Warning (v.18)

In verse 17, Paul encouraged the Philippians to imitate godly examples - those who live in accordance with the gospel of Christ. But now, in verse 18, he offers a sharp contrast. There are some, he says, who do not walk in the same manner. They are not examples to follow - but warnings to heed. This next verse is deeply emotional and sobering: *"For, as I have often told you before and now tell you again even with tears, many live as enemies of the cross of Christ."* (Philippians 3:18)

Paul is not speaking in anger, but in anguish. This is a pastoral cry, not a theological debate. His heart is breaking - not only because some have turned from the truth, but because their lives are leading others astray. Let's look closely at what this verse teaches us about spiritual discernment, gospel fidelity, and the dangers of abandoning the way of the cross.

"As I have often told you…" - A Repeated Warning

Paul begins by reminding the Philippians that this is not the first time he has addressed the issue. *"As I have often told you before…"* These are not new concerns. Paul has consistently warned the church about people who distort the gospel, and he repeats the warning here.

This teaches us something critical: some truths need to be repeated. We often grow weary of hearing the same message, but spiritual health depends on constant reminders of the dangers around us.

Like a shepherd who never tires of warning his sheep about the wolves, Paul returns again and again to this concern. Why? Because these enemies of the cross are not far away. They are nearby. Their influence is real. Their message sounds convincing.

False teaching and false living are not just external threats - they often rise from within the community of faith. This is why we must remain vigilant, returning again and again to the true gospel.

"And now tell you again even with tears..."

Perhaps the most striking part of this verse is the phrase, *"even with tears."* Paul does not speak these words with a clenched fist, but with a broken heart. He is not gloating over the downfall of others. He is not puffed up in self-righteousness.

His tone is not cold or calculating - it is *weeping*. This is what makes Paul's warning so powerful. It flows from deep sorrow, not judgmental superiority. These tears show us his pastoral heart - a heart that grieves over those who have rejected the truth and endangered others in the process.

This is important for us to understand: Truth and tears go together in gospel ministry. We must be bold in speaking the truth, but we must also be broken-hearted over those who reject it. Truth without love hardens. Love without truth deceives. But truth *with* love - truth spoken with tears - mirrors the very heart of Christ.

Let us ask ourselves today: Do we speak the truth with compassion? Do we grieve over those who wander from the gospel? Or have we become indifferent - or even smug - in the face of their lostness?

"Many live as enemies of the cross of Christ..."

Here is Paul's warning in plain terms: *"Many live as enemies of the cross of Christ."* Notice carefully - he does not say they are enemies of religion, or enemies of morality, or even enemies of Christ in name. He says they are enemies of the cross. This is crucial. What does it mean to be an enemy of the cross?

The cross represents:

➢ *Sacrifice*: Jesus giving His life for sinners.

➢ *Grace*: Salvation not by works, but by the blood of Christ.

➢ *Humility*: The Son of God humbling Himself to the point of death.

➢ *Repentance*: A call to die to self and live to God.

To be an enemy of the cross, then, is to reject this message. It is to oppose the way of self-denial, grace, and surrender. It is to promote a message of self-indulgence, self-righteousness, or self-salvation.

Many commentators believe Paul is referring here to two kinds of people:

1. *Legalists* - Those who reject the sufficiency of Christ's sacrifice and try to earn salvation through works (like the Judaizers Paul warned about earlier in chapter 3).

2. *Libertines* - Those who claim to follow Christ but live in open rebellion, indulging the flesh and denying the need for holiness.

Both are enemies of the cross - because both distort the gospel. One denies the sufficiency of grace. The other denies the call to obedience. One adds to the cross. The other mocks it.

In our time, we see the same threats:

➤ Some preach a gospel of performance - do more, try harder, be good enough.

➤ Others preach a gospel of permissiveness - God loves you, so do whatever feels right.

But the true gospel says: *Come and die. Be forgiven. Be made new. Follow Jesus.* Philippians 3:18 reminds us that we live in a spiritual battlefield. Not everyone who claims Christ truly follows Him. There are many who walk in ways that oppose the cross, and their influence is real.

But Paul's example shows us how to respond:

➤ *With truth* - we must expose error and call people back to the gospel.

➤ *With tears* - we must speak with compassion, not condemnation

➤ *With discernment* - we must be wise in who we imitate and follow.

➤ *With hope* - because the cross still saves, still transforms, and still calls.

As we continue in this passage, Paul will point us to the ultimate hope - the return of Christ and the glory to come. But for now, let us hear the warning with open hearts and tearful resolve.

Our True Home and Ultimate Hope (vv.19–21)

Having warned with tears about those who live as enemies of the cross in verse 18, Paul now describes their lifestyle and destiny with sobering clarity: *"Their destiny is destruction, their god is their stomach, and their glory is in their shame. Their mind is set on earthly things."* (v.19)

This verse provides a four-fold profile of the spiritually lost - those who may appear religious or respectable, but whose lives are shaped by self and not by Christ.

a. "Their destiny is destruction"

The final end of those who reject the cross is ruin. Paul is not exaggerating or being dramatic. He is describing eternal separation from God - not simply physical death, but spiritual condemnation. Paul's warning is clear: it matters how we live. It matters whom we follow. It matters whether our lives are shaped by the cross or opposed to it.

b. "Their god is their stomach"

This phrase refers not only to physical appetites, but to unrestrained desires of every kind. To make a god of the stomach is to serve one's own cravings - whether for food, pleasure, wealth, power, or recognition.

Paul is highlighting a life governed by self-indulgence, not self-denial. These individuals worship comfort, not Christ. Their desires dictate their choices.

c. "Their glory is in their shame"

In other words, they boast about what they should be ashamed of. What the Bible calls sinful, they call liberating. What God condemns, they celebrate. This is more than moral failure - it is moral inversion.

This is painfully relevant in today's world. Many take pride in what dishonours God. But this is not new. Paul saw it in the Roman world. We see it in ours.

And the church must respond not by retreating into silence or self-righteousness, but by faithfully proclaiming the truth and living lives of holiness.

d. "Their mind is set on earthly things"

This is the root issue. Their minds - hearts, values, priorities - are fixated on the things of this world. They measure success by material gain, approval by popularity, and purpose by personal happiness. They live with no reference to eternity, no awareness of God's judgment or presence, and no hunger for spiritual transformation.

This is the defining feature of those who are enemies of the cross: they are earthbound. Life is about the here and now. The eternal is ignored, if not rejected.

"But our citizenship is in heaven" (v.20)

Paul now makes a dramatic turn - from those whose minds are fixed on the earth to those whose identity is rooted in heaven. *"But our citizenship is in heaven."*

This is one of the most powerful identity statements in the entire New Testament. Paul reminds the Philippians - and us - that we do not ultimately belong to this world.

Our truest allegiance, our deepest loyalty, and our eternal identity is not found in a nation, culture, or earthly system. It is found in heaven.

This statement would have carried special significance for the Philippians. As residents of a Roman colony, they were proud of their Roman citizenship - even though they lived far from Rome itself. Their culture, laws, language, and dress reflected their Roman identity.

Paul uses this as an analogy: just as Philippians were Roman citizens living abroad, we are heavenly citizens living on earth. Our conduct, our values, our loyalties - everything about us - should reflect our heavenly home.

This truth challenges us to evaluate our priorities:

> ➢ Do we live like citizens of heaven?

> ➢ Do our goals, relationships, and decisions reflect eternal realities?

> ➢ Or are we more influenced by culture than by Christ?

Being a citizen of heaven means we live as ambassadors on earth. We represent the interests of our King, speak the language of grace, and live with the values of the kingdom of God.

"And we eagerly await a Saviour from there..." (v.20b)

Paul continues: *"... And we eagerly await a Savior from there, the Lord Jesus Christ."* As citizens of heaven, we don't just look back to the cross - we look forward to the return of our King. Our hope is not grounded in human progress or political reform. It is anchored in the promise that Jesus is coming again.

This eager waiting is not passive. It is hopeful, joyful, and active. It shapes how we live now. We live in expectation - not fear or despair - because the One who saved us is the One who will return to complete our redemption. This contrasts powerfully with those described in verse 19. Their destiny is destruction, our destiny is transformation. While their minds are set on earth, ours are lifted to heaven. We live not for what is fading, but for what is eternal.

"Who... will transform our lowly bodies..." (v.21)

Paul ends this passage with a breathtaking promise: *"...who, by the power that enables him to bring everything under his control, will transform our lowly bodies so that they will be like his glorious body."* This is the final hope of every believer. When Christ returns, He will not only renew the world - He will renew us.

Our frail, mortal, perishable bodies will be transformed to be like His resurrected body - immortal, glorious, and fit for eternity.

The same power that created the universe and upholds all things will accomplish this. Jesus will subdue everything under His authority. No force of sin, death, or decay will resist Him. He will bring it all into submission - and in doing so, He will complete the salvation He began in us.

This promise is intensely personal and it is also profoundly comforting:

> For those who suffer physically, it offers the hope of healing.

> For those who battle sin, it offers the hope of victory.

> For those who mourn, it offers the hope of resurrection.

This is not myth or metaphor. It is the future reality for all who belong to Christ.

Conclusion:

In this passage, Paul calls the church to live according to their true identity and future destiny. He contrasts the enemies of the cross - whose lives are shaped by earthly desires, and citizens of heaven, whose hope is anchored in Christ's return.

So how then should we live in light of this?

> **With discernment** – knowing that not all who claim Christ follow Him.

> **With integrity** – letting our lives reflect our heavenly citizenship.

➤ **With anticipation** – looking forward to Christ's return with hope.

➤ **With perseverance** – standing firm as we await final transformation.

Our hope is not in this world. Our Saviour is coming. And when He comes, everything broken will be made whole, everything lowly will be lifted, and we will be made like Him. Let us live each day as citizens of heaven - faithful, joyful, and steadfast - until the day He comes again.

11. UNITY IN CHRIST

Philippians 4:1-9 *"Therefore, my brothers and sisters, you whom I love and long for, my joy and crown, stand firm in the Lord in this way, dear friends! I plead with Euodia and I plead with Syntyche to be of the same mind in the Lord. Yes, and I ask you, my true companion, help these women since they have contended at my side in the cause of the gospel, along with Clement and the rest of my co-workers, whose names are in the book of life.*

Rejoice in the Lord always. I will say it again: Rejoice! Let your gentleness be evident to all. The Lord is near. Do not be anxious about anything, but in every situation, by prayer and petition, with thanksgiving, present your requests to God. And the peace of God, which transcends all understanding, will guard your hearts and your minds in Christ Jesus.

Finally, brothers and sisters, whatever is true, whatever is noble, whatever is right, whatever is pure, whatever is lovely, whatever is admirable - if anything is excellent or praiseworthy - think about such things. Whatever you have learned or received or heard from me or seen in me - put it into practice. And the God of peace will be with you."

Introduction: Unity and Stability in Turbulent Times

Paul has just finished an inspiring passage in chapter 3, reminding us of our heavenly citizenship and our ultimate hope in Christ's return. Now, as he turns to chapter 4, he brings those heavenly truths to bear on very earthly concerns. In this short but powerful section, he moves from grand theological themes to practical church life. His words are filled with urgency, affection, and wisdom. The church in Philippi was faithful and generous, yet even they were not immune to division.

In these three verses, Paul calls the church to stand firm, to stay united, and to help restore peace where it has been fractured. The message is clear: as we wait for Christ's return, we must be a people marked by perseverance, humility, and reconciliation.

"Therefore, my brothers and sisters…"

Paul begins in verse 1 with a deeply affectionate greeting: *"Therefore, my brothers and sisters, you whom I love and long for, my joy and crown…"* This is one of Paul's most emotionally rich introductions. He piles on terms of endearment, showing us the depth of his relationship with the Philippian believers:

> *"Brothers and sisters"* - A reminder of their shared spiritual family.

> *"Whom I love and long for"* - Reflecting his deep and emotional connection and his desire to be with them.

> *"My joy and crown"* - Expressing how proud and grateful he is for their faith and partnership.

For Paul, the Philippians are not just another church. They are his joy - the fruit of his ministry - and his crown, his reward in Christ. Their faithfulness brings him profound delight. This is a valuable reminder for us.

Christian community is not simply an organizational necessity - it's a spiritual family. Our love for one another should be heartfelt, not formal. Our concern for each other's growth and wellbeing should be personal, not distant.

In a world increasingly marked by division and superficial relationships, the church is called to something deeper: *gospel-shaped affection* that builds bridges and strengthens bonds.

"Stand firm in the Lord in this way..."

Paul's primary exhortation in verse 1 is this: *"Stand firm in the Lord in this way, dear friends!"* This phrase echoes the military language often used in Paul's letters. To *"stand firm"* is to hold your ground - to remain unmoved in the face of pressure, opposition, or temptation. But notice the key phrase: *"in the Lord."* This isn't about personal willpower or stubborn resistance. It's about being rooted in Christ.

We stand firm not in ourselves, but in the truth, presence, and power of the Lord. This call to spiritual stability is not new in the letter. Paul has already urged the Philippians to:

➤ *"Conduct yourselves in a manner worthy of the gospel..."* (1:27)

➤ *"Stand firm in the one Spirit..."* (1:27)

➤ *"Work out your salvation with fear and trembling..."* (2:12)

Now he reinforces the call to perseverance. And what follows in verses 2 and 3 gives us insight into how that perseverance looks - especially in the context of community conflict.

"I plead with Euodia and I plead with Syntyche..."
A Painful Disagreement

In verse 2, Paul addresses a specific issue: *"I plead with Euodia and I plead with Syntyche to be of the same mind in the Lord."* This is one of the rare moments in Paul's letters where he names individuals in the context of a personal disagreement.

We know very little about Euodia and Syntyche, but a few things are clear:

- They were likely prominent women in the Philippian church.

- They had been faithful coworkers in the gospel (as v.3 implies).

- Their disagreement was significant enough to threaten the unity of the church.

Paul uses repetition for emphasis: *"I plead with Euodia... I plead with Syntyche..."* He is not taking sides. He is not addressing one as the guilty party and the other as the victim. He appeals to both equally, urging them to be *"of the same mind in the Lord."* This phrase - *"same mind"* - is one Paul has used earlier in the letter:

- *"Make my joy complete by being like-minded..."* (2:2)

- *"In your relationships with one another, have the same mindset as Christ Jesus..."* (2:5)

The goal is not uniformity of opinion, but unity in attitude - a Christlike mindset of humility, love, and mutual submission. Every church will experience disagreement. What matters is how we handle it. Do we allow division to fester? Do we choose pride over peace? Or do we, like Paul, plead for reconciliation grounded in the Lord?

"Yes, and I ask you, my true companion..." – The Role of the Peacemaker

In verse 3, Paul brings in a third party: *"Yes, and I ask you, my true companion, help these women since they have contended at my side in the cause of the gospel..."* This unnamed *"true companion"* is asked to step in and assist in the reconciliation process. Paul is not content to leave the situation unresolved. He invites a trusted leader to come alongside Euodia and Syntyche and help restore peace.

This is a powerful picture of pastoral care and church leadership. Sometimes, reconciliation requires the help of a mature believer - a peacemaker who can mediate with wisdom and grace.

The church is a family. When one part of the body is in conflict, the whole body is affected. That's why Paul includes this appeal in a public letter. He wants the church to care for one another - not just through encouragement, but also through accountability. Importantly, Paul honours the two women involved. He reminds the church that these women have *"contended at my side in the cause of the gospel."* They are not troublemakers or immature believers - they are gospel coworkers who need help navigating a painful moment. The goal is not blame, but restoration.

In these three verses, Paul offers a compelling vision for Christian community:

➢ A place of deep affection and mutual love.

➢ A place of steadfast faith rooted in the Lord.

➢ A place where disagreements are not ignored but addressed with grace.

➢ A place where leaders and members work together for peace.

Unity in the church is not automatic - it must be pursued. It takes humility, courage, and help from others. But it is worth the effort. As we reflect on this passage, let us ask:

➢ Am I standing firm in the Lord?

➢ Am I contributing to unity or division in my church?

➢ Am I willing to help others reconcile?

➢ Am I cultivating relationships marked by grace, truth, and shared purpose?

This is what it means to be the body of Christ. To stand firm - not just side by side, but heart to heart - in the Lord who unites us all.

Rejoice and Rest - Living in the Peace of God

Having just urged unity and peacemaking in verses 1-3, Paul now shifts the focus inward. How can believers not only live at peace with one another, but also live at peace within themselves - especially when life is uncertain, stressful, or painful? Philippians 4:4-7 contains some of the most quoted and cherished verses in the New Testament. In just four short verses, Paul gives a roadmap for a joy-filled, prayerful, and peaceful life, grounded not in circumstances, but in Christ.

These verses are not sentimental slogans - they are spiritual instructions for how to live faithfully in a broken world. They call us to a mindset and lifestyle that is radically different from the surrounding culture. They summon us to rejoice, to pray, and to rest in God's presence and promises. Let's explore each verse and uncover the truths that can transform our daily lives.

"Rejoice in the Lord always. I will say it again: Rejoice!" (v.4)

Paul begins this section with a double command: *"Rejoice in the Lord always. I will say it again: Rejoice!"* This is not a suggestion or a mood-based encouragement - it is a command. And it's not the first time Paul has said it. Rejoicing is a consistent theme in this letter:

➤ *"I always pray with joy…"* (1:4)

➤ *"Rejoice with me!"* (2:18)

➤ *"Rejoice in the Lord!"* (3:1)

But here in chapter 4, Paul makes it explicit: *"Always."* That's a challenging word. How can we rejoice always? What about grief, pain, loss, or disappointment?

The key lies in the phrase *"in the Lord."* Our rejoicing is not based on fluctuating circumstances, but on an unchanging relationship. The Lord is always present, always good, always sovereign, always loving. We may not rejoice in what's happening, but we can rejoice in who He is.

This kind of joy is deeper than happiness. It's not shallow or manufactured. It flows from knowing that, in Christ, we are loved, secure, forgiven, and never alone.

Rejoicing in the Lord is a spiritual discipline. It requires intentional focus on the truth of the gospel. It grows when we give thanks, worship regularly, and reflect on God's character. That's why Paul repeats it: *"I will say it again: Rejoice!"* We need the reminder. Joy is not natural in a fallen world - it must be chosen, cultivated, and guarded.

"Let your gentleness be evident to all. The Lord is near." (v.5)

After calling the church to rejoice, Paul exhorts them to live with *"gentleness."* This word can also be translated as *"reasonableness," "graciousness,"* or *"moderation."* It refers to a spirit that is not harsh, defensive, or combative. It's the opposite of a quarrelsome or anxious heart. Paul is saying: *"Let your calm, humble, gracious spirit be visible to everyone around you."*

This kind of gentleness is desperately needed in today's polarized and reactive world. When everyone is quick to speak, slow to listen, and eager to argue, a gentle Christian stands out as a powerful witness.

Paul adds a motivation for this gentleness: *"The Lord is near."* This may refer both to God's nearness in presence and to Christ's imminent return.

> *If God is near,* we don't need to defend ourselves, panic, or control others. His presence sustains and protects us.

> *If Christ is coming soon,* we don't need to prove ourselves right or win every argument. Our hope is secure, and time is short.

Gentleness flows from confidence in God. It is a fruit of the Spirit (Galatians 5:23) and a mark of Christlikeness.

"Do not be anxious about anything..." (v.6a)

Now Paul addresses one of the greatest struggles in life: anxiety. He says: *"Do not be anxious about anything."* At first glance, this might sound dismissive or unrealistic. How can anyone not be anxious - especially when life is filled with pressures, responsibilities, and unknowns?

But Paul is not scolding or simplifying. He is offering a way out of anxiety - not by denying problems, but by redirecting our response. The Greek word for *"anxious"* here means to be pulled apart - to be mentally and emotionally torn in different directions. That's a vivid picture of what anxiety does. It distracts, divides, and drains us. Paul's instruction is clear: *Do not let anxiety rule you.* Instead, he tells us what to do in its place.

"But in every situation, by prayer and petition, with thanksgiving, present your requests to God." (v.6b)

The antidote to anxiety is prayer. Paul says to bring *everything* to God - not just spiritual needs, but every situation. Whether it's work, health, relationships, finances, or decisions, nothing is too small or too big to bring before Him.

He uses three words to describe our communication with God:

> *Prayer* – a general word for communion with God.

> *Petition* – focused requests, asking God for specific help.

> *Thanksgiving* – expressing gratitude for what God has done and is doing.

This threefold approach reflects the depth of a healthy prayer life:

> We *connect* with God in relationship (prayer).

> We *ask* God for what we need (petition).

> We *thank* God for His faithfulness (thanksgiving).

When we respond to anxiety with prayer, we are not simply managing stress - we are relocating our trust. We are shifting our burdens from our own shoulders to God's. And when we include thanksgiving in our prayers, it reshapes our perspective. Gratitude reminds us of God's past faithfulness and renews our hope in His future provision.

"And the peace of God, which transcends all understanding, will guard your hearts and your minds in Christ Jesus." (v.7)

This is the result of prayerful trust: the peace of God. This peace is not just the absence of conflict or tension. It is an inner stability and calm that comes from knowing God is in control. Paul says this peace *"transcends all understanding."*

That means it doesn't always make sense. It's not logical by human standards. It can exist even in the middle of chaos, grief, or waiting. It is supernatural.

And this peace doesn't just comfort - it *guards*. The Greek word Paul uses is military in nature, referring to a sentry or soldier keeping watch. The peace of God then becomes a protector over our inner life.

> - It guards our *hearts* - our emotions, desires, and affections.
> - It guards our *minds* - our thoughts, fears, and assumptions.

But notice the final phrase: *"in Christ Jesus."* This peace is not generic or self-generated. It is found only in Him. Relationship with Christ is the key to rest for the soul.

Philippians 4:4-7 offers us a vision of a different kind of life:

> - A life marked by *joy*, regardless of circumstances.
> - A life marked by *gentleness*, in the face of conflict.
> - A life marked by *prayer*, not anxiety.
> - A life marked by *peace*, not panic.

This is the fruit of a life centred in Christ. It does not come automatically or effortlessly - but it is available to every believer who chooses to trust, pray, and rejoice in the Lord. Let us learn to rejoice always, to pray in every situation, and to rest in the peace that surpasses all understanding.

Think and Live What Is True (vv.8-9)

Paul has been building a vision for Christian steadfastness. In verses 1-3, he urged unity and reconciliation. In verses 4-7, he gave us a path to peace through joy, gentleness, and prayer. Now in verses 8-9, he brings the message to a climax by shifting from our actions to our attitudes - from outer circumstances to inner thought life.

Paul understood that what we think about matters. Our mindset shapes our emotions, our actions, and ultimately, our spiritual maturity.

That's why these final verses of our passage are so powerful and practical. Paul offers us a kind of mental filter, a spiritual lens through which all our thoughts must pass.

"Finally, brothers and sisters..." – The Turning Point

Paul signals a transition: *"Finally..."* Not necessarily the end of his letter, but the final summary of this section. He wants to leave the Philippians with something that ties together all he's said about standing firm, rejoicing, praying, and trusting God. And what he gives us is not another command - but an invitation to think differently.

"Whatever is true, whatever is noble, whatever is right, whatever is pure, whatever is lovely, whatever is admirable - if anything is excellent or praiseworthy - think about such things." (v.8)

This is not a random list. It's a carefully crafted pattern meant to redirect our mental habits and fill our minds with things that nourish the soul and honour God.

"Whatever is..." - A Thought Life Worth Pursuing

Let's look briefly at each of the qualities Paul lists. These are the things we are to *"think about"* - which in the Greek means to dwell on, meditate on, give sustained attention to.

a. *True* - That which aligns with God's reality: This includes the truths of Scripture, the gospel, and all that is honest and reliable.

In a world filled with lies, distortions, and half-truths, believers must cling to what is truly true - not what is trending, sensational, or emotionally comfortable.

b. *Noble* - Honourable and dignified: These are thoughts that elevate rather than degrade. To think nobly is to fill our minds with that which is worthy of respect - thoughts that uplift our hearts and help us live as people of integrity.

c. *Right* - Just and righteous: This means focusing on what is morally right - what reflects the character and justice of God. We should think about decisions, behaviours, and systems that promote righteousness and fairness.

d. *Pure* - Morally and spiritually clean: In an impure world, we must guard our minds against pollution. Purity isn't naivety - it's a heart that refuses to be entertained by what defiles. We are called to meditate on what is untainted by sin.

e. *Lovely* - Pleasing and beautiful: This refers to things that inspire love, peace, and harmony. Not everything that is true is lovely - some truth is hard. But lovely things stir affection for God and others. They make our hearts tender and joyful.

f. *Admirable* - Worthy of praise or approval: These are thoughts that commend what is excellent in character and conduct. They celebrate virtue rather than vice.

g. *Excellent or praiseworthy* - Moral and spiritual excellence.

Paul concludes with a catch-all phrase: *"if anything is excellent or praiseworthy..."* He is urging us to pursue excellence in our thought life - to avoid mediocrity or mindlessness in what we consume, contemplate, and celebrate. In summary, Paul wants believers to develop mental habits that form godly character. Right thinking leads to right living. A healthy mind is essential to a holy life.

"Whatever you have learned... put it into practice." (v.9)

Paul shifts in verse 9 from contemplation to action: *"Whatever you have learned or received or heard from me or seen in me - put it into practice."* This verse highlights a critical principle: Christian growth involves both knowledge and application.

Paul is not simply calling the Philippians to admire his teaching - he is urging the Philippians to imitate his life. He points to what they have *learned* from him (his teaching), *received* (his mentoring), *heard* (his preaching), and also what they have *seen* (his example). Then he says: *"Now live it out in your daily lives."*

This is not arrogance from Paul - it's pastoral responsibility. Paul knows that example is a powerful teacher. His life - marked by faith, suffering, service, and joy - is a living chapter. And he invites others to follow Christ by following him. Every mature believer should be able to say the same. Not because we are perfect, but because we are pursuing Christ with sincerity and consistency.

The call to *"put it into practice" reminds* us that the Christian life is not merely mental - it is practical. We must take the truth we believe and live it out in daily habits, relationships, and decisions.

"And the God of peace will be with you." (v.9b)

Paul ends with a promise. In verse 7, he promised that the peace of God would guard our hearts. Now he promises that the God of peace Himself will be with us. This is more than emotional comfort. It is divine companionship.

When we think rightly and live obediently, we experience not only God's peace, but His presence.

- ➤ He walks with us.
- ➤ He strengthens us.
- ➤ He comforts us.
- ➤ He anchors us.

This promise is a fitting conclusion to the call to stand firm. No matter what challenges the Philippians face -whether from within or without - they can move forward with courage, knowing the God of peace is with them.

Conclusion:

Philippians 4:8-9 is a call to intentional living. It reminds us that we must take responsibility for our thoughts and our actions.

- ➤ What we dwell on will shape what we become.
- ➤ What we admire will shape what we pursue.
- ➤ What we practice will shape the fruit we bear.

Paul's vision for the Christian life is not passive or abstract. It is concrete and compelling. He wants us to think deeply, live boldly, and walk closely with the God of peace. So let us fill our minds with what is true, noble, right, pure, lovely, and admirable. Let us put into practice what we've learned from Christ and those who follow Him. And let us walk in the unshakable peace that only God can give.

This is what it means to stand firm in the Lord - with our hearts guarded, our minds renewed, and our lives aligned with the gospel.

12. THE SECRET OF CONTENTMENT

Philippians 4:10-23 *"I rejoiced greatly in the Lord that at last you renewed your concern for me. Indeed, you were concerned, but you had no opportunity to show it. I am not saying this because I am in need, for I have learned to be content whatever the circumstances. I know what it is to be in need, and I know what it is to have plenty. I have learned the secret of being content in any and every situation, whether well fed or hungry, whether living in plenty or in want. I can do all this through him who gives me strength.*

Yet it was good of you to share in my troubles. Moreover, as you Philippians know, in the early days of your acquaintance with the gospel, when I set out from Macedonia, not one church shared with me in the matter of giving and receiving, except you only; for even when I was in Thessalonica, you sent me aid more than once when I was in need. Not that I desire your gifts; what I desire is that more be credited to your account. I have received full payment and have more than enough. I am amply supplied, now that I have received from Epaphroditus the gifts you sent. They are a fragrant offering, an acceptable sacrifice, pleasing to God. And my God will meet all your needs according to the riches of his glory in Christ Jesus. To our God and Father be glory for ever and ever. Amen.

Greet all God's people in Christ Jesus. The brothers and sisters who are with me send greetings. All God's people here send you greetings, especially those who belong to Caesar's household. The grace of the Lord Jesus Christ be with your spirit. Amen."

A Personal Word from Paul

As Paul draws his letter to a close, he shifts from theological instruction and ethical exhortation to a warm expression of gratitude.

But even in this personal section, profound truths emerge about Christian living. The Philippians had renewed their financial support of Paul during his imprisonment, and he writes to thank them - not as some beggar grateful for a handout, but as a shepherd rejoicing in their partnership and generosity. Yet, rather than simply say *"thank you,"* Paul uses this moment to testify about his own journey into true contentment.

This passage stands as one of the clearest teachings in the Bible on how to find peace - not by changing our circumstances, but by being transformed in the midst of them. As we examine Paul's words, we discover what it means to rejoice in God's provision and live with spiritual contentment, regardless of the ups and downs of life.

"I rejoiced greatly in the Lord..." (v.10)

Paul opens this section with joy: *"I rejoiced greatly in the Lord that at last you renewed your concern for me."* His joy is not in the money or material gift itself - but *"in the Lord."* The phrase is critical. Paul always anchors his emotions and responses in his relationship with Christ. The gift was the occasion, but Christ was the source of his joy.

Paul's language here is nuanced. He says, *"at last you renewed your concern for me,"* but then immediately clarifies: *"Indeed, you were concerned, but you had no opportunity to show it."* There's no hint of rebuke or disappointment. Instead, Paul acknowledges that the Philippian believers had always cared about him, but due to circumstances - distance, lack of communication, political restrictions, or timing - they hadn't been able to express it until now.

The Greek word for "renewed" (*anethalete*) is a botanical term, meaning to bloom again. Paul is saying: *"Your concern has flowered again."*

Their support was not a new emotion, but a re-blooming of long-standing affection. This shows us that true Christian generosity is often seasonal. There are times when we are able to give more freely, and times when we are not. But the heart of partnership remains. Paul's response models grace, patience, and gratitude - not entitlement or manipulation.

"I am not saying this because I am in need..." (v.11a)

Paul goes on to clarify his motive: *"I am not saying this because I am in need..."* He wants to make it clear: his joy is not rooted in finally receiving what he lacked. He is not rejoicing because his physical needs were finally met. In fact, his next words are stunning: "For I have learned to be content whatever the circumstances." Here we begin to see the heart of Paul's spiritual maturity. He had discovered the secret to stability and peace, not in abundance, not in predictability, not in success, but in contentment.

The word "learned" suggests a process. This wasn't instant. Paul didn't receive contentment like a lightning bolt. He *learned* it - over time, through experience, through hardship and dependence on God. That's encouraging for us. Contentment is not a personality trait. It's not reserved for a few naturally optimistic people. It's a spiritual discipline, cultivated in the school of trust and surrender.

"I have learned to be content whatever the circumstances." (v.11b)

This is one of the most radical statements in the New Testament. Paul's contentment wasn't limited to seasons of plenty or peace. It extended to every circumstance. Consider Paul's life: He had been beaten, imprisoned, shipwrecked, betrayed, and often left without food, clothing, or companionship. And yet, he could say with full integrity: *"I have learned to be content."*

Contentment, in biblical terms, does not mean resignation or passivity. It does not mean we don't pursue change or growth. Rather, it means our inner peace is not controlled by outer conditions.

In this, Paul echoes the wisdom of Proverbs 30:8–9: *"Give me neither poverty nor riches but give me only my daily bread. Otherwise, I may have too much and disown you… or I may become poor and steal…"* True contentment flows not from having everything, but from trusting God in everything.

Learning Contentment in Every Season (v.12)

Paul expands on his experience: *"I know what it is to be in need, and I know what it is to have plenty. I have learned the secret of being content in any and every situation, whether well fed or hungry, whether living in plenty or in want."*

Paul's contentment was not theoretical. He had lived through both abundance and scarcity, feasting and fasting, comfort and crisis.

His point is clear: neither poverty nor prosperity defines his peace. Both have dangers. Poverty can lead to despair. Prosperity can breed pride or false security. But Paul had learned to live above these extremes by anchoring his heart in something deeper. He calls this a *"secret."*

In Greek, the phrase suggests initiation into a mystery - something not immediately obvious or accessible. That secret is revealed in the next verse and will be the focus of Part 2.

But the lesson is very clear: Contentment is not found in circumstances. It is always learned through communion with Christ.

The Church's Example and the Christian's Hope

As Paul shares these insights, he is not boasting but offering an example to the Philippians - and to us. In a world driven by consumerism, comparison, and constant dissatisfaction, the church is called to model a different way.

Paul's words challenge our assumptions:

➢ That more stuff will make us happy.

➢ That comfort is the highest goal.

➢ That success equals spiritual blessing.

Instead, we see that Christ is enough. We can learn to be content in plenty or in want, in joy or sorrow, because our treasure is eternal and our hope is secure.

Philippians 4:10-12 gives us the foundation for a life of peace and joy that transcends circumstances. Paul's journey reminds us that contentment is not automatic, but it is possible.

➢ It begins with *rejoicing in the Lord* - not in outcomes or possessions.

➢ It grows as we *learn through life's highs and lows*.

➢ It is sustained by *trust in God's character and provision*.

This kind of life is countercultural - but deeply freeing. When we are no longer slaves to our circumstances, we are free to live with gratitude, purpose, and peace. As we continue, we will discover the heart of the secret Paul refers to in verse 13.

Strength Through Christ Alone (v.13)

Philippians 4:13 is one of the most quoted verses in the Bible: *"I can do all this through him who gives me strength."*

It appears on coffee mugs, t-shirts, posters, and social media posts. It is used by athletes, entrepreneurs, performers, and dreamers. For many, it has become a kind of Christian slogan for personal achievement.

But context is everything. Paul is not talking about winning competitions or accomplishing grand goals. He is not saying, *"With Jesus, you can do whatever you set your mind to."* Rather, he is explaining the secret of contentment - how he has learned to be at peace in every situation, whether in plenty or in want.

This verse is not about self-empowerment. It's about Christ-dependence. It's not about striving. It's about abiding. Let's dive deeper into this profound verse and discover what it truly teaches us.

"I can do all this..." – Anchored in Context

The verse begins: *"I can do all this..."* Many translations (especially older ones) render it: *"I can do all things..."* which, when taken out of context, sounds limitless. But the NIV rightly translates the phrase in light of the preceding verses: *"I can do all this."*

What is "this"? The *this* refers to everything Paul has just described in verses 11 and 12:

> ➢ Being brought low and being lifted up.
> ➢ Having abundance and suffering need.
> ➢ Being well fed and going hungry.

In other words, Paul is saying, *"I can face any circumstance - good or bad - and remain content."* The focus is not on achieving anything imaginable, but on enduring everything faithfully.

This is important because it protects us from misusing Scripture to promote unrealistic expectations. God never promised that we would be able to accomplish every goal, win every game, or avoid hardship. But He has promised that in every circumstance, His strength is sufficient.

"Through Him..." – The Source of Strength

The second part of the verse is the key: *"through him who gives me strength."* Paul is not celebrating his own toughness or resilience. He is not saying, "I've trained myself to be unshakable." He is declaring that Christ is the source of his inner strength.

This phrase could also be translated: *"through the one who empowers me,"* emphasizing the ongoing, active nature of Christ's enabling presence.

The Christian life is not about trying harder but depending deeper. Christ's presence in us is not passive; it is empowering. He gives us:

➢ *Spiritual strength* to resist temptation.

➢ *Emotional strength* to persevere through sorrow.

➢ *Mental strength* to trust in uncertainty.

➢ *Relational strength* to forgive and love difficult people.

And most of all, He gives us the strength to be content - even when life does not go as planned. Paul is speaking from experience. When he was shipwrecked, imprisoned, beaten, and abandoned, Christ's strength sustained him.

When he was lifted up as a leader or cast down as a criminal, Christ never left him. Paul's contentment was not because life was easy - but because Christ was enough.

Contentment Is Not Natural - It's Supernatural

What Paul is describing here is not natural. The natural response to hardship is frustration, worry, or despair. The natural response to abundance is pride, greed, or complacency. But Paul had found a better way - a supernatural strength that allowed him to remain steady in both extremes.

This echoes what Jesus said in John 15:5: *"Apart from me, you can do nothing."*

Paul understood this. He didn't just believe in Christ - he relied on Christ. He had discovered that his sufficiency was not in himself, but in the living, present Christ who dwelled in him by the Spirit.

This is why Paul could write elsewhere:

- *"To live is Christ and to die is gain."* (Philippians 1:21)
- *"We have this treasure in jars of clay to show that this all-surpassing power is from God and not from us."* (2 Cor 4:7)
- *"When I am weak, then I am strong."* (2 Cor. 12:10)

This paradox - strength through weakness - is at the heart of Christian discipleship.

The Practical Power of Christ's Strength

So how does Christ give us strength in everyday life? This verse is not only theological; it is profoundly practical. Christ empowers us to:

- *Endure suffering* without losing faith.
- *Wait patiently* when prayers seem unanswered.
- *Say no to temptation*, even when it costs us.

> *Forgive others* when we've been deeply wounded.

> *Serve joyfully* when we feel tired or unseen.

> *Live generously* when resources are tight.

> *Worship sincerely* even in sorrow.

Christ's strength is not a surge of adrenaline; it is a steady grace that enables us to stay faithful when everything else says give up.

Learning to Rely on His Strength

If Paul learned to be content through Christ's strength, then so can we - but we must learn it. That means making intentional choices:

> *Choosing prayer over panic.*

> *Choosing worship over worry.*

> *Choosing Scripture over self-help.*

> *Choosing dependence over independence.*

We learn Christ's strength by walking with Him daily - not just during crises. We draw from His strength as we abide in His Word, pray in the Spirit, and walk in obedience. And just like Paul, we discover that His grace is sufficient.

So what is the secret Paul learned? It is this: Christ is enough. Whether in hunger or abundance, in chains or freedom, in obscurity or recognition - Christ sustains us. He strengthens us.

He empowers us not to escape life's hardships, but to endure them with peace and purpose. Philippians 4:13 is not a motivational quote. It is a radical confession of faith - that the believer can face anything, not because they are strong, but because Christ is stronger.

Let us take this truth to heart today. When we are tempted to grumble, compare, despair, or strive, may we instead say with Paul: *"I can do all this through Him who gives me strength."*

Generosity, Glory, and Grace (vv.14–23)

Paul began his letter to the Philippians with gratitude, and now, as he concludes, he circles back to it - ending with thanksgiving, encouragement, and a rich benediction.

In these final verses, we not only see Paul's personal appreciation for the Philippians' generosity, but also his theology of giving, his confidence in God's provision, and his unwavering focus on the glory of God. There's no better way to conclude this letter of joy, unity, and contentment than with a celebration of gospel partnership and the enduring grace of Jesus Christ.

"Yet it was good of you to share in my troubles." (v.14)

Although Paul has just declared that he is content in every circumstance and strengthened through Christ (vv.11–13), he quickly adds a gracious clarification: *"Yet it was good of you to share in my troubles."* This shows Paul's pastoral sensitivity. He wants the Philippians to know that their gift was not overlooked. Their generosity mattered - it was a tangible expression of their love and partnership.

The word *"share"* here is from the Greek root *koinonia*, the same word Paul used earlier for fellowship and partnership in the gospel. This wasn't just financial help - it was actually a participation in Paul's suffering, a joining in his mission, a sign of true Christian solidarity. The Philippians didn't just send a gift - they stood with Paul when it was risky to do so. They supported him when others remained silent. That kind of loyalty reflects the heart of Christ.

**"Not one church shared with me... except you only."
(vv.15–16)**

Paul reminds them of their unique and consistent support: *"Moreover, as you Philippians know, in the early days of your acquaintance with the gospel, when I set out from Macedonia, not one church shared with me in the matter of giving and receiving, except you only; for even when I was in Thessalonica, you sent me aid more than once when I was in need."*

This was not a one-time donation - it was a pattern of faithful support. From the earliest days of their conversion, the Philippians took the initiative to provide for Paul's needs, even when other churches did not.

What stands out is their missional mindset. They didn't just give out of emotional response or obligation. They gave because they were invested in the spread of the gospel. They saw themselves not as spectators, but as co-workers.

This challenges us today. Are we giving out of convenience, or out of conviction? Do we see generosity as worship? Do we view our resources as instruments in the hands of God to advance His kingdom?

"Not that I desire your gifts..." (v.17)

Once again, Paul clarifies his motives: *"Not that I desire your gifts; what I desire is that more be credited to your account."* Paul wasn't manipulating them for financial gain. His concern was not with what he would receive, but with what they would gain spiritually through their generosity.

He uses the language of accounting - *"credited to your account."* Paul sees their giving not just as a transaction, but as an eternal investment.

Jesus taught the same principle: *"Store up for yourselves treasures in heaven."* (Matthew 6:20) Every act of generosity, done in faith and for the glory of God, is credited in heaven. Paul is rejoicing not only in their help, but in their spiritual fruitfulness. Giving is not loss - it is gain. Not necessarily materially, but eternally.

"They are a fragrant offering... pleasing to God." (v.18)

Paul describes their gift in deeply spiritual terms: "I have received full payment and have more than enough. I am amply supplied... They are a fragrant offering, an acceptable sacrifice, pleasing to God." He draws from Old Testament imagery, where sacrifices offered in worship were called *"a pleasing aroma to the Lord."* (Leviticus 1:9)

In Paul's view, the Philippians' financial gift was not merely practical - it was worship. It was an offering made not to Paul, but to God Himself. This reminds us that our generosity - whether to missionaries, local churches, or people in need - is ultimately given to God. And when it is done in faith, it brings Him pleasure. Worship is not just singing songs - it includes how we handle our money, how we bless others, and how we support gospel work.

"And my God will meet all your needs..." (v.19)

This is one of the most comforting promises in Scripture: "And my God will meet all your needs according to the riches of his glory in Christ Jesus."

Notice the <u>certainty</u>: *"will meet"* - not *might meet.*

Notice the <u>scope</u>: *"all your needs"* - not just spiritual, but emotional, physical, relational, and financial.

And notice the <u>source</u>: *"according to the riches of his glory in Christ Jesus."* Not out of God's riches - but according to them.

That means God's provision is not limited, but lavish. He supplies not sparingly, but in abundance. This promise is not a blank check for luxury or indulgence. It is a guarantee that as we give in faith, God will never leave us lacking in what we truly need. He is a faithful provider.

Paul isn't promising that every want will be fulfilled, but that every need will be met - in ways that are wise, timely, and glorifying to God.

"To our God and Father be glory for ever and ever." (v.20)

Paul now bursts into doxology - an eruption of praise: *"To our God and Father be glory for ever and ever. Amen."* All of this - Paul's ministry, the Philippians' generosity, God's provision - it all leads to one ultimate goal: the glory of God. This is the heartbeat of Paul's life.

Everything exists for God's glory. The church's mission, the believer's joy, the world's redemption - it all culminates in praise to the Father. When we give, when we serve, when we trust - we glorify God. And that is the highest purpose of our lives.

Final Greetings and Benediction (vv.21–23)

Paul concludes with final greetings: *"Greet all God's people in Christ Jesus. The brothers and sisters who are with me send greetings. All God's people here send you greetings, especially those who belong to Caesar's household."* Even in prison, Paul is surrounded by believers. And he makes special mention of *Caesar's household* - a reference to those in the imperial court who had come to faith. Even in the heart of the Roman Empire, the gospel was bearing fruit.

Paul ends with the words he began with: *"The grace of the Lord Jesus Christ be with your spirit. Amen."*

Grace is the first word and the final word. That's because it is the foundation of our salvation, the strength of our sanctification, and the source of all joy and contentment.

Conclusion:

As we conclude this 12-part journey through Philippians, we are left with a powerful image: a man in chains, overflowing with joy, thanking a generous church, and giving all glory to God. Paul's life and letter show us that true contentment is not found in circumstances, but in Christ. It is possible to rejoice always, to trust God deeply, to love others sacrificially, and to live for what truly matters.

Let us remember:

- *To live is Christ.*
- *To die is gain.*
- *We press on toward the goal.*
- *We stand firm in the Lord.*
- *And we do all things through Him who gives us strength.*

May our lives, like the Apostle Paul's, be always marked by grace, generosity, and glory - until the day we finally see Jesus face to face.